William Hepworth Dixon

The Switzers

Third Edition

William Hepworth Dixon

The Switzers
Third Edition

ISBN/EAN: 9783337152116

Printed in Europe, USA, Canada, Australia, Japan

Cover: Foto ©ninafisch / pixelio.de

More available books at **www.hansebooks.com**

THE SWITZERS.

BY

WILLIAM HEPWORTH DIXON.

𝕿𝖍𝖎𝖗𝖉 𝕰𝖉𝖎𝖙𝖎𝖔𝖓.

LONDON:
HURST AND BLACKETT, PUBLISHERS,
13 GREAT MARLBOROUGH STREET.
1872.

TO

THE RT. HON. W. E. FORSTER, M.P.,

THIS PICTURE OF

A FREE PEOPLE

IS

INSCRIBED.

PREFACE.

'In from Vevey?' hails an English voice at Neufchatel, where trains from Vevey and Lausanne meet trains from Bern and Zürich on their way to Paris.

'Yes; and you—from Bern?' replies a New-York voice.

'From Bern. You had a good time?'

'Yes; it rained Niagara; but the lakes are lovely and the mountains absolutely grand.'

'Saw anything of the Switzers?'

'Eh? You mean the boys who lead your mules, and cook your meals, and tie you up in ropes? Not much. Somehow, you hardly notice them. Why not? Well, now you ask me why—

I think it is because they are so quiet, and get on with what they have to do so well.'

'These people, when you come to know them, are as much worth study as their alps and lakes.'

'Indeed! Then tell us all about them.'

6 St. James's Terrace,
  New Year's Day, 1872.

CONTENTS.

CHAP.		PAGE
I.	MOUNTAIN MEN	1
II.	ST. GOTHARD	10
III.	PEOPLING THE ALPS	18
IV.	THE FIGHT FOR LIFE	29
V.	RAIN AND ROCKS	40
VI.	TEUTON AND CELT	52
VII.	THE COMMUNES	62
VIII.	COMMUNAL AUTHORITIES	71
IX.	COMMUNAL GOVERNMENT	79
X.	CANTONS AND HALF-CANTONS	86
XI.	CANTONAL RULE	99
XII.	CANTON ZÜRICH	109
XIII.	PURE DEMOCRACY	119
XIV.	A REVOLUTION	130
XV.	POPULAR VICTORIES	140
XVI.	THE LEAGUE	150
XVII.	THE FEDERAL PACT	159
XVIII.	JESUITS	169
XIX.	PILGRIMAGE	181

CONTENTS.

CHAP.		PAGE
XX.	CONVENT AND CANTON	192
XXI.	ST. MEINRAD'S CELL	203
XXII.	FEAST OF THE ROSARY	214
XXIII.	LAST OF THE BENEDICTINES	226
XXIV.	CONFLICT OF THE CHURCHES	237
XXV.	SCHOOL	247
XXVI.	DEMOCRACY AT SCHOOL	254
XXVII.	GENEVA	262
XXVIII.	SCHEME OF WORK	274
XXIX.	SECONDARY SCHOOLS	285
XXX.	SCHOOL AND CAMP	296
XXXI.	DEFENCE	306
XXXII.	THE PUBLIC FORCE	317
XXXIII.	IN THE FIELD	327
XXXIV.	OUT AGAIN	340
XXXV.	A CROWNING SERVICE	349

THE SWITZERS.

CHAPTER I.

MOUNTAIN MEN.

'WE are a folk apart, we mountain men,' a Switzer says—a Switzer who has seen the world, and learnt in many lands to know the ways of man and nature—as we watch the sun go down behind a screen of domes and peaks. 'What say you, Sister Agnes; are we not a folk apart?'

A Nun from Sion, in the Canton Valais, with a ruddy cheek and pair of southern eyes, this Sister Agnes is a pilgrim of the season, on her way to Meinrad's Cell, the famous chapel of Our Lady of the Anchorites in Canton Schwyz. She is the chance companion of a day. We found her sitting at a wayside cross; we took her up, for she was sore of foot and slight of frame. While we were dining at an inn, she wandered to the ice-caves, lost her way, and fell. At length we found her, weak with pain, and brought her to this mountain-pass.

An Engineer from Bern, a man of thirty-five, with bearded chin, broad brow, and pair of cold blue eyes, the Switzer is on public duty in these mountains; armed with rule and chain, with drill and mallet; to interrogate these crests, to tap these rocks, to span each beck and fall, to note each curve of alp, and try if science cannot find some means of saving the great wreck of life and land below, by guiding, and controlling at their sources, the St. Gothard floods.

Fair types of South and North, of Celtic and Teutonic Switzerland, are these companions of the way; the girl from Sion and the man from Bern; one warm and feminine, with a drooping brow, and eyes that wait on nature and solicit saintly help; the other strong and masculine, with head thrown back, and eyes that peer into the granite, and rely on man's own wit and strength. The girl, with rosary dangling from her girdle, is a servant of the Cross; the man, with mallet in his lifted hand, a genuine son of Thor.

Too busy with her thoughts to answer him,

the Nun, her eyes bent steadily on the west—a sky all amber, blush and blue—runs nimbly through her beads, while words, inaudible to man, appear to part her lips in prayer.

'Just note,' he adds, a touch of pity in his tone, 'how far we are a race apart. We have no kings, no subjects; every man is free. We have no noble class, no pauper class, no standing army, no official church. We have no language of our own. We have no common code. We have no public debt. No man among us owns the best part of a canton, as a Russian prince the best part of a province, and an English duke the best part of a shire. Nine men in ten are owners of the soil they graze and plough.'

'You are a race apart!'

'The earth on which we build and plant is not a stretch of vineyards, orchards, cornfields, pastures, dropping towards the sea on every side, with hardly any break of waste. We dwell among the crags and clouds. Our flats are mostly water and our slopes are mostly ice. Your plains lie basking in the summer, while our heights are swept by storm. Your river-beds are loam; our river-beds are grit. You dreamers by the water-side have but to wait on Nature, while we watchers by the mountain-side must take her gifts by force.'

'It is by natural law that mountains make the mountain men?'

'How else? Man acts on Nature in his way, as Nature acts on man in her way, till the two great spirits of the earth grow like each other, even as a man and wife who live in peace grow like each other year by year. Among the vines and olives in Italian gardens men are soft, poetic, phosphorescent; no less full of fire than they are fond of change. Among the pines and larches of Valaisian glaciers men are hardy, patient, dumb; as slow to fume and flash as they are hard to bend and break.'

'Yea, some are hard to bend and break!' sighs Sister Agnes, who has told her beads, and now sits looking into space.

'As men in plains take up a drift and ply,' the Engineer goes on, 'so men on mountain-tops take up a drift and ply. Our drift is to be silent, sleepless, prompt; for we lie down with danger at our doors, and we must rise to meet it when the moment comes. At dusk you see a cottage on a shelf of rock; a hut in which the shepherd churns his milk; a bit of soil in which he grows his herbs; a patch of grass on which his heifers browse; a simple cross at which his urchins pray. At dead of night a tremor passes through the mountain side; a slip of earth takes place; a cry which no one hears rings up to heaven. At dawn there is a lonely shelf of rock above, a desolate wreck of human hopes below.'

'We strive too much,' again sighs Sister Agnes, bending to his tale: 'we fight for earthly things when we should give our minds to heavenly things. What are we doing in this Year of Pilgrimage? Preparing to bore holes through living rocks, and ride to Rome in railway trains, when he who is the father of all Christian men is held a prisoner in his house by disobedient sons!'

'You folk who live in flats and hollows,' says the man of science, glancing at the Nun with curious smile, 'build towns, in which you dally with the graceful arts; while we, who cling like limpets to our rocks, raise châlets far and wide, from which we tend our flocks, in which we find a shelter from the fiery clouds. You have the fig, the citron, and the vine; we have a treeless waste, with long, coarse grass, and mosses which the goat and chamois dare not crop. Dame Nature nurses us to different ends. To you is given the genius to construct the marble fane, the royal castle, and the fretful town; to us, the timber chapel, the industrious household, and the lowly thorpe.'

'A little lowliness of heart would do us good,' exclaims the Nun—the golden sunset on her face—'if we could only learn to know our place, and give to Heaven the things of Heaven!'

A smile that seems to say—if ever smile has meaning—'I should like to kiss that nonsense from your lips,' plays round his delicate mouth and sparkles in his cold blue eyes. A moment afterwards he adds:

'In every zone, so far as I have seen, the mountain races are a free, a pastoral, an unchanging people. Men who come from cities find us rough, and fancy we are dull. All mountain races love the past; suspect new words, new things, new men; and harden like the hills in which their lives are spent. Their fundamental laws are few and slowly formed; as slowly formed as they are stoutly held. A hill-tribe stands upon their ancient ways.'

'God and His angels are the same for evermore,' responds the Nun.

'Turn where you list, and take the lesser with

the greater heights; the crests of Snowdon and Ben Nevis, through the Pyrenees to Monte Negro and the Julian Alps; in every zone you find this rule—the mountain-people stand aloof from what is new and strange, while those who live on plains and by the sea, are apt to change their laws and creeds from year to year. The hill-tribes of Judea kept their covenant, while the tribes of Jordan and Esdraelon fell away. Those Medes who never changed a law, descended from the Caspian alps; those Greeks who sought new things from day to day, were dwellers by the Ægean sea.'

'You think the sea has much to do with man's desire for change?'

'It is the cause. A man who looks on water grows like water, and a man who looks on alps grows like an alp.'

'Yet, tell me, is it not the rule that alpine tops are barren of great men?'

'It is so. Let the worst be said that can be said in truth. No prophet ever comes from mountain-top; no poet, thinker, warrior of the foremost order, comes from mountain-top. All gifts of hand and tongue, all services of art and science, are in less demand with us than in the streets of busy towns, where every one is seeking after something new, and chiefly for his personal good. We know it; nay, we make it so.'

'You do not want great men in your republic?'

'No; we want good men, not great men. In our system, what you call great men can have no part; they would disturb us, perhaps destroy us. A republic is a league of equals, not a company of general officers and men-at-arms. A great man is a monarch. If a Cæsar should arise among us, we might have to kill him. In his craft, each man among you strives to be the first, and you applaud his efforts, even when they fail. You like a man to be a duke. Your maxim is, be first in your own class. Such maxims are not ours: we have no ducal spirit in these alps. We are a band of brothers, but without an eldest born. Our rule is—All for each, and each for all —the oath of Grütli—our unwritten code. All teaching has with us this end in view, that no one shall grow up into a man till he has learnt to rank the public weal above his private gain.'

'We set the peace of earth above the grace of Heaven,' observes the Nun.

'You train your youth,' the Bernese engineer proceeds, 'by contrast and contention; we by sympathy and mutual help. You urge each scholar to surpass his fellows; we forbid all effort to disturb the line. You like to see one lad above his class, for you have put your trust in dukes and chiefs. We notice such a thing with pain, and try to make our boys regard each other in the school-room as their right and left hand files. Your method brings out special strength, and makes one giant to a hundred dwarfs. Again, you take but scanty notice of the weak; you dote on strong majorities: and push your brethren who are weak in number, to the wall. You have the conqueror's spirit in your camp. You seek opinions which are strong, and clothe those strong opinions with the garb of public law. We have a tender feeling for the weak. We break the force of our prevailing wind by groynes, by dykes, and by dividing walls; that is to say, by giving to each Canton and each Commune in our country separate and substantial powers; to every Canton equal votes, to every Commune local life. You see we are a folk apart!'

CHAPTER II.

ST. GOTHARD.

THE sun is sinking on a cloud of summits as we pace the road which, winding up the Siedeln alp, and vaulting over by the Furka, weds the two great valleys of the Rhone and Reuss, and brings the Simplon pass into connexion with the Gothard pass.

A mist is rising in our front from horn and glacier, from the Grimsel ridges, from the Gelmer snow-fields, from the Handeck falls, a mist which swells the solar disk and turns the flame to fire. Athwart this thickening haze the light is flashing into lengths and streams, and the white clouds above these lengths of light are rolling into curves and crowns. The colours melt and deepen as we gaze. A moment since the tints were amber, rose, and blue; but while we speak that amber burns to gold, that pink grows crimson, and that blue is purple, brown and black. Afar off, in the Bernese Oberland, two pyramids of earth, —the Schreck-horn and the Finster Aar-horn,— part these ever-widening waves; two dark and mighty cones, which tower above the highest wreaths of cloud.

Our right is bounded by the Rhone glacier; a scarp of frozen ice; here rough with shales of slate, there dark with drifts of dust. So near us lies this shining fall that we can peer into the rents and watch the play of green and rosy light within them. Down below, the surface of the glacier has been smoothed and rounded by the noon-day heat; along our level it is jagged and broken by the midnight chill. A ravine passes to our left—a sombre ravine, which ascends the ridge on which the Muttbach feeds; and over this dark parting of the ridges rise the Mutt-horn, Shaf-berg, Tell Alp, Saas-horn; while beyond these peaks, and partly hidden from our sight, extend those granite walls which press the summer back upon Italian lakes. Below these masses, in the groove between the Mutt-horn and the Grimsel, flow the waters of the Rhone—here lost to sight among the rocks, there flooding out among the trees and fields— past Oberwald and Obergestelen, then through long green reaches, lit with roof and spire—sweet notes of life and home in the stern desert of an alpine night. Up north and west, above the Grimsel, spread the crests and gulfs to which no spring, no autumn, ever comes; a realm where it is always either frost or fire; where chain is laid on chain, and peak is piled on peak; with domes and falls of ice, with sweeps and drifts of snow, and pinnacles of rock too sharp for either flying mist or driving rain to clutch. Beyond the Grimsel stretch the Gauli glacier, the lesser and the greater Grindelwald glaciers, the Kander glacier, the two Aar glaciers, the Lötschen glacier, the Münster glacier, and the Aletsch glaciers, hanging on the sides and dripping at the feet of secondary alps; while high above these seas of ice roll up vast fields of granulous snow, too high for sun to melt; and over these white fields, the humps and teeth of Jungfrau, Wetter-horn, and Mönsch, with yon twin pyramids of earth, the Schreck-horn and the Finster Aar-horn, which divide the flashing lines of light—as though they stood in arms, two mountain kings, to guard their brides and captives from a bold, crusading sun.

Yet nobler than such wintry masses, and

to larger use and purpose, swells the group of heights on which we stand—the crown of the St. Gothard chain, the central range of Europe, where her valleys run to meet each other, whence her rivers rise and flow to east and west, and over which the Frank and Teuton pass to Lombardy, while the Italian climbs towards Germany and France.

This central group of the St. Gothard chain, like other mountain systems, has her trough, her platform, and her cardinal peak.

Her trough is Urseren—the Uri valley—once an alpine lake, like that of Wallenstadt in form and size, but lying in a loftier bed. The lowest hamlet in this hollow stands four thousand and six hundred feet above the sea. A green but treeless basin, into which the snow comes down with the September chills, and nestles in the clefts and gullies till the latest day of June, this trough is watered by the Reuss, a stream which, rising near the Furka, brawls past Re Alp, Hospenthal, and Andermatt, until it issues from the trough near Teufelstein. Some firs creep meekly up St. Ann's—an alp round which the last few flights of the St. Gothard road wind up—but they are dwarfed in size and thinned in mass by the exceeding cold. Some herdsmen, guides, and muleteers, who live by aiding people on their way, have built in Urseren the thorpes in which a passenger finds food and fire.

Her platform is not sharply marked by nature; for the ridges flow into each other, and the ravines break these ridges here and there — as at St. Gothard, Six Madun, the Devil's Bridge, and Längis Grat; but still, an oval, somewhat roughly drawn, with Re Alp for a central point, would sweep the edges of this platform. Draw a line from Rhone-stock by the Gersten-horn, across the valley of the Rhone to Saas-horn and Lucendro, round the Lago Sella to Six Madun, and thence to Toma, Aldez, Süisen, Teufelstein, and by the Batzberg and the Spitzberg, through the Winter glacier to the Rhone-stock. In this oval, seven miles wide and fourteen long, are crowded peak, and source, and pass. The Rhone wells out below the Galen-stock; the Rhine flows downward from the Toma lake; the Reuss goes rattling past the Siedeln Alp; the Toccia starts beneath the Saas-horn; the Ticino drops from Lago Sella. All the greater lakes are fed from this one crown of earth; Lake Constanz from the

Six Madun; Lake Leman from the Galen-stock; Lago Maggiore from the Sasso di Gottardo. Three drops of rain, delivered from one drifting cloud, might fall into the Rhone, the Toccia, and the Rhine, and after filtering through Lake Leman, Lago Maggiore, and Lake Constanz, might run forward on their several ways into the sea, past Avignon, Cremona, and Cologne.

Her cardinal peak is Galen-stock—the peak now towering on our right—a fount of light and beauty in this sombre realm, which ancient shepherds, coming up the valleys of the Rhone and Reuss in search of fortune, called the Pillar of the Sun. He is the Saul of the St. Gothard group—above the tallest of his brethren: Gerstenhorn, Lucendro, Mutt-horn, Spitz-berg, Six Madun—though all these mountains are of Anak breed. Three glaciers hang about his hoary neck and shiver down his sturdy sides; the Tiefen glacier on his northern flank, the Siedeln glacier on his southern flank, and the Rhone glacier (which has many feeders) on his western flank. These glaciers drip by different ravines, and descend to different seas. Above his summit floats a canopy of cloud, from under which at times leap fire, and wind, and hail, those rival demons of this upper air, which shake and daze the earth in their plutonic and magnetic strife. About his feet, low down among the ruts and wrecks of ice, lie caves of wondrous beauty and uncounted wealth. Three years ago a cave was entered by this Tiefen glacier, when the noblest crystals in the world were found. The rock was topaz. Fragments lay about in heaps, each broken piece a hundred pounds, two hundred pounds, in weight. Some fifteen tons of topaz were removed from this great hiding-place of nature in a single year. What sage can count the marvels yet in lurking near this pillar of the Sun?

There—spent at last—the fiery orb is gone! Dark domes of cloud are rising round his couch. A faint green tinge still charms the upper sky, and specks of silver touch the highest peaks; but all the ravines at our feet are veiled, and all the secondary alps are lost to sight. At such a time one feels how poets in the guise of shepherds, with an eye on straying goat and heifer, learned to call this central point of their converging tracks the pillar of the Sun. This peak is still a coronet of fire.

Far down, in either of the valleys in our front and rear, as far as Biel in front, as far as Andermatt in rear, the herdsmen raise their eyes at sunset and at sunrise towards this signal in the clouds, the first to catch, and last to hold, that radiance which is light and life to man. At Biel you see the villagers come out, long after sunset in their narrow trench, to watch the glowing tints die off this point, and augur from the depth of gold the fortunes of another day. At Andermatt the rustics turn to it at dawn, while yet the roadway up the Ober Alp, the ruined tower of Hospenthal, the fringe of forest on St. Ann's, are buried in profoundest gloom. Above Re Alp and Bülen-stock there is a flash, a star, a comet, which expands and colours to a pinnacle of flame. It is the pillar of the Sun, the central peak of the St. Gothard group.

CHAPTER III.

PEOPLING THE ALPS.

'We mount and mount,' the Bernese adds as we return into the châlet, numb with cold, but deep in the great question as to how these alps are crossed and kept; 'we rise each year, and soon the summits will be crowned.'

Excelsior!

A man who finds a pass and plants his foot upon a peak, secures that pass and peak. A second follows where he led; his trail is worn into a track. Then guides and porters come to ply their trade. A shed is built, a cross set up; in time that shed becomes an inn, that cross becomes a spire. A deed once done is easy to repeat. It is the first step only that is hard to face. When Whymper scaled the Matter-horn, and fortune took four lives as fine, all Europe shuddered at the tragic tale; and he who came down victor from the rocks, would never front that task again. Yet he had shown the way, and three days after his ascent, and while the bodies of the dead were still unfound, four guides went up and gained the perilous cone. Next year came two ascents, and in the one next after, five. Now boys and girls go up that cone in sport. A week ago, two English damsels clambered to the ledge from which poor Hudson fell. Already there are hints of future roads. One track is worn from Zermatt up the German front; another from La Breil up the Italian front. Two-thirds of the way from Zermatt to the peak, a hut has been erected by the guides. You find there wood and wraps, with pans for warming food, and shelter from the sudden storm. A few years more, and what is now a lonely hut will be a pleasant, populous inn.

A man in search of food and fuel gains some ledge, and caps it with his hut and fence. The scrub is fired around him, and the tarns are drained of their abundant ooze. As Nature owns her master, she retires before him step by step. The glacier drips and wastes, the snow-fields melt to mist, the larches creep beyond his axe, and plum and walnut flourish where those larches lately grew.

Not long ago, you found the firs and larches at Sierre, in Canton Valais; now you have to seek for them at Brieg. A vine will sprout to-day where pines would hardly cling some years ago. At Pontresina corn is grown; at Chiamut corn is also grown; and yet the lower of these alpine hamlets stands as high above the sea as Cader Idris would be piled upon the head of Skiddaw.

Two hundred years since Rigi was an unknown solitude. Old writers never name this mountain, though its beauty was the same in olden times as now; from base to kulm a dream of scenic and botanic wealth; with snowy ridge and slope above, with oleander, fig, and balsam near the water edge. At Vitznau, in the first week of October, when the Bürgen-stock and Ennet-horn are white with winter, grapes are hanging from the frames, and flowers and fruits are in Sicilian wealth and waste. On shelves of rock grow walnuts, and above them fir and larch. At Kaltbad there are ferns; and over Kaltbad sloping grassy alps; and then a stretch of snow-field to the kulm, with its unrivalled view of mountain, lake, and plain. Yet all this beauty is for man a thing of yesterday. The first who mentions Rigi was a seeker after rare and lovely plants. He only wandered at her base and by the edges of her shining lakes. He left the Scheideck and the kulm alone, as heights too poor for him to name. Some cattle, straying up the hill, drew shepherds after them, when huts were built for shelter, and a citizen of Arth, a hamlet on Lake Zug, erected for these lonely men the Chapel of Our Lady in the Snow. This chapel of Our Lady made the Rigi-famous; for miraculous cures were heard of far and wide; and pilgrims came from Altdorf and Luzern to pray for health. A flight of thirteen stages—as on Carmel—led from Unteres Dächli to Our Lady's shrine; at every stage a pilgrim knelt and prayed, and took in mountain air, and felt himself a better man. In time, the cloisters, and the hospice, and the chapel of St. Malchus, were erected on the Rigi slopes; but years on years elapsed before a hut was built for travellers near the kulm. Not until 1848 had any one the courage to erect an inn. This inn was but a small affair, and yet the landlord's neighbours thought him mad. His house was much enlarged in 1856; and fifteen years later we are driving railway engines almost to the chapel of Our Lady in the Snow.

'You mark,' observes the Engineer, 'how we

are climbing up. No sooner is that railway engine up the Rigi than a plan is laid for throwing it across the ridge, and down the other face, to Goldau, with a branch to Arth. Five years ago the passage from Luzern to Meyringen was by a bridle-path across the Brünig; now there is a mountain-road, with busy traffic, and a scatter of good houses to the highest woods. But we are not content with such a road. We mean to have a railway line across the Brünig pass, and perhaps a branch to that black lake in which, according to the legend, Pilate drowned himself. Already surveys have been made; a year hence men will be at work with spade and pole; and in a little while the iron horses will be tearing past Brienz and Unterseen for Thun. You know the Schynige Platte below the Faul-horn, with its famous glimpse of Lauterbrunnen and the Grindenwald. It is a level higher than the Rigi-kulm. Among my papers are the plans for a new railway to the summit of this Platte, and surveys for a branch line to the Faul-horn! Three years hence that line will be at work.'

'Ah me!' sighs Sister Agnes, shrinking from the Engineer, whom she is ready to regard as one possessed, 'we kick this dust about our feet and fancy we are taking heaven by storm! More fit that we should fall upon our faces and confess our sins!'

'You nurse the spirit of your pilgrimage,' I venture to remark.

'Do not,' she says, with downcast eyes, 'believe that all of us are mad with this vain pride of life. Some souls are found, even yet, who will not sell their birthright in the future heavens for such a mess of herbs. A short time hence will be our Festival of the Rosary. Come over into Canton Schwyz, and meet the pilgrims at Our Lady's Shrine.'

'In no long time,' retorts the Engineer—as fervent in his science as the Sister in her faith—'our ridges will be pierced, our lakelets will be drained. At three great centres we are tapping through the granite walls; the Splügen, the Lukmanier, the St. Gothard; in a dozen years the railway trains will roll from Hamburg and Vienna through these mountains on their way to Rome. Here runs the road from London to Brindisi, Cairo, and the Indian seas. A straight line drawn from London to Bologna passes through the hospice of St. Gothard, and a bee line is the pathway for an iron horse. Already we are turning to our lakes in search of land. Before the Dutch drew Haarlem, we had drained the floods from Linth and Giswyl, and had won five hundred acres from the lake of Lungern. We have a scheme for lowering the too high levels of the Jura lakes, arresting inundations of the Aar, and bringing the vast marsh of Seeland under spade and plough. Five million francs are voted for this purpose by the League. But local jealousies step in. Each Canton and each Commune has some petty cause to serve; but some dark night a flood will drown them into reason, and a hundred thousand acres will be gained. Our lakes should yield a million acres. Leman might be lowered one-third. Such lakes as Sarnen, Sempach, Löwertz, Greifen, may be drained away.'

'Your science figures out the work of ages.'

'Pardon me, of years. Why, men now living knew a time when there was not one road for wheels across these alps. It is not easy even yet to keep an open road upon the Furka, which is higher than the Gemmi and St. Gothard passes; for the snow lies deep about this châlet till the end of June. Some seasons it is later: in the middle of July this year the depth was twenty feet. These sheds, from which the shales are carried once a-week, are but of yesterday. Not long since you could walk from Oberwald, in the Rhone valley, to Re Alp in the Reuss valley, and scarcely find a shelter from the storm. A dismal hut stood near the glacier—now it is a good hotel —but not a second house was to be seen. The refuge near the Tiefen glacier was not built, and now you have a road from Brieg to Chur, across the Furka and the Ober Alp, with an hotel at every turn.'

'You put your engineer before the monk,' says Sister Agnes; 'yet methinks the saints came up into these heights before the men of science found their way.'

'My sister, you are right,' replies the Engineer; 'for Gothard was a saint, and Carlo Borromeo was a saint.'

The early monks were engineers, path-finders, inn-keepers, and guides. The hunters who came up erected huts of refuge, like the huts on Zermatt now—the hut of logs or stones, without a keeper, lending you a shelter from the sudden storm, the darkening night, and the bewildering snow, but nothing more—no fire, no food, no rest, no help. Some monk comes up, intent on flying from himself and from the world. He lights a fire, prepares a couch, and brings in stores of bread. The refuge is a hospice, and the keeper is a holy man. What then? Some helper in his kitchen, with an eye to gain, erects a shed outside the walls, provides more dainty fare and lodging, and invites the passer-by to taste his food and test his beds. The hospice is an inn. We find these several stages on the summit of St. Gothard, where the refuge, hospice, and hotel stand side by side. Some refuges may pass at once into the stage of inns. Below the Tiefen glacier, stands a refuge, where you groom your horse and drink good Veltner wine. A man has come to live there who is not a saint, and in another season he may offer you a dinner and a bed. A few miles farther down you find a hospice at Re Alp, in which live Father Hugo and a troop of girls. That house is called a hospice: but in wine and waiting-maids you might mistake it for a merry country inn.

'This Father Hugo,' laughs the Bernese, 'is our Friar Tuck. Your fine old Capuchins are dying off; their trade is passing into other hands. The dogs have had their day.'

The Sister drops her head and tells her beads.

At first this climbing up is hard, but men

get used to what is hard, and when their spirits are in tune, the task is easier than it seemed at first. When Balmat clomb Mont Blanc the effort all but killed him. Every step he took was strange; the unseen perils chilled his veins; and when he came down, sore and scorched, he sank into his bed. The doctor roused him by a word. He, too, would scale the mountain. Balmat rose at once, drew on his boots, and faced the danger with a lightened heart. Next year De Saussure followed, with a village in his wake; and after them came all the world, who filled the valley with their presence, up to Col de Balme. The Montanvert, the Flégère, and the Mer de Glace, grew famous. Sheds were raised, and guides were trained, to serve the climbers. Near the Montanvert one Blair, a Scotchman, built that hut, from which the poet Göthe looked upon the Sea of Ice. Not only Chamounix, but Sallanches, Servoz, and Argentière, feel the shock of a new life. Schools, churches, and hotels spring up. Each col and glacier has a separate inn. The Tête Noir is rounded; the Hôtel de Cascade is opened; and the gorge of the Trient bridged. New tracks are opened up Mont Blanc, and a descent is found towards Italy. Young damsels clamber to the top, and now the feat is little but a jest and show. A frame of planks was taken to the Grands Mulets not eighteen years ago. It was supposed to be a feat; and now there is a scatter of stone houses on the several roads; one house on the Aiguille du Goûter; two houses on the Grands Mulets; inns at Pavillon, La Balma, Chapin, Mottet; châlets at Ferret, Forclaz, and the Allée Blanche.

'It is a fight for life,' the Bernese man of science cries; 'but men have won it, and will win it to the end. In no long time there will be inns at Grands Mulets, and in a hundred years the summit of Mont Blanc may be a town.'

CHAPTER IV.

THE FIGHT FOR LIFE.

THIS fight for life is not unfrequently conducted to the death. Man cannot climb so high, but some great charge of wrath seems hanging over him; a beetling crag, a stream of stones, a cataract of ice, a moving field of snow; and higher yet than these wild demons of the earth, those still more ruthless spirits of the air—the flash that rends his roof, the wind that strips his trees, the flood that drowns his land.

Against each messenger of ill, a man must hold a separate watch—the avalanche, the lightning, and the deluge; and must learn to brave each danger when it comes, alike by flush of noon and in the dead of night.

'When we have won a field from nature,' says the Engineer, 'we carefully entrench the ground, and try to hold what we have gained against her, even though she hurls her avalanches on our heads.'

'Your science tells you how to cope with avalanches?'

'For the most part—yes. But in these mountains, men are so perverse! By right no avalanche should ever fall on thorpe and field. If such an evil comes upon us, it is much our fault; but people who believe in saints and not in science take no trouble to protect themselves against the sliding weight. They leave their safety to the saints, and winter takes them in her shroud of snow.'

'They leave themselves defenceless by their want of thought in cutting down the pines?'

'The man who breaks his flail to boil his kettle is a sage compared to men like those of Selva, Cumiasca, and a hundred hamlets in these Celtic alps. These peasants burn the props that shore their house. In cutting down the pine-woods, they entreat the avalanche to crush them. Think of Selva—buried in the snow three several times—and every time by her own act and deed.'

Midway from Ober Alp to Sedrun, in the Fore Rhine valley, lies this thorpe of Selva; an Italian village, as the name implies; a group of thirty houses, more or less; a small white chapel nestling in the cliff; a scratch of green stuff growing in the flints; a strip of pasture running by the stream; and hanging overhead a fringe of firs. Above the village, towers the Milez Alp, sheer up into the air a thousand feet. This Milez is connected with the Crispalt, an enormous field of snow, from which the dry and granulous flakes roll down in streams. The village houses, built of logs, are strongly knit, and every shingle on the roof is weighted with a slice of rock.

A crisp and lightsome people dwell in Selva; rustics of Italian type, with ruddy flesh, dark hair, and tawny hands; a folk who read no books, who see no papers, and who boast no arts, excepting how to feed their kine and press their cheese, to sing their village songs and dance at village feasts. You find in Selva—as in every other Commune—schools and books; but these things are exotics in the land. The schools are poor, the books are lives of saints. The Pater has his office, and some patriot in a bigger hut may have a copy of Professor Condrau's journal, the Gazetta Romonscha. Condrau's journal, printed in the neighbouring town of Dissentis, is dear to Celtic patriots; for the Professor sets himself to show that the

Teutonic Switzer is a sort of Kindli-fresser, who devours the children of his fellow Celts. No other books and papers trouble the repose of Selva; for these southern people are not weighted with much care of life. They only want to eat and drink, to court and wed, to feel the love of wife and child, to hear that God is with them, and to sleep at last among their sires. Their ways are old-world ways. They never miss an office in their church. They speak that peasant Latin which was heard in the Campagna ere Augustus reigned in Rome. Their houses have a rustic reek, their thoroughfares a southern grime. Not only in their swarthy fronts and flashing eyes, but in their jewelled ears, both men and women have a menace and a memory of those ancient homes, from which they came into these alps as masters of the world.

These men of Selva love their valley with a languid and abiding love. The strips of grass are scant; the hauls of trout are rare; the sheaves of grain are few. The valley is too narrow for much grass, the flood too rapid for much trout, the country-side too damp and lofty for much corn. For Selva, low as she may look if you peer down upon her from the Ober Alp, stands higher in the list of hills than Snowdon would be with Ben Nevis on her back. But still these Celtic rustics, with their ancient farming skill, contrive to coax from her ungrateful soil some golden sheaves. A patch of ground is chosen with a southern face; a troop of youngsters pick it clear of stones; a bank of scrub and logs is made to wall it up; and when the seed is thrown into the soil, a groyne of slabs and stones is thrown along the higher rim, but slant-wise from the alpine scarp (as we in in England groyne the sea), to turn all floods of rain and rolling earth and stones aside. The shoots are never high, the ears are never full; but when the air grows chill at noon they cut the stalks and tie them up on frames of wood to dry. Corn ripens fast when it is cut.

A brisk and antique race, with Celtic fire and indolence, these rustics would be poor and merry on their lofty perch, were not the Milez alp and Crispalt horn above them, charged with seas of snow and ice. They live beneath these wintry ledges as their countrymen near Naples live beneath the fiery cones. A heavy fall of snow is doom. The shoulder of the alp gets overcharged; the lower edge gives way; the upper crest obeys the slide; and then the great white Death comes down on roof-tree, chapel, field, and flock.

'Why don't you quit the thorpe?' you ask a peasant who has seen his hut destroyed three several times.

'We cannot quit the spot,' he says: 'it is our home; the land is ours; where should we find another place?'

'The world is wide, this valley of the Rhine is long. There must be other alps to graze.'

'But none like Selva. Here we live in peace. We keep our laws and customs; speak our native tongue, and have no fear of chop and change. If we go down to Trons we meet the Germans; if we go to Ilanz we shall find the heretics. We stick to Selva while she sticks to us.'

'But you have sometimes thought of changing quarters?'

'Only once; and only part of us were minded to remove. I was a youngish man; my lad, now driving yonder team, was in his crib; but old men who could speak of things ere I was born, all said it was the biggest slide of snow yet seen at Selva. All our cottages were crushed. Our church was buried in the snow, and nearly all our goats and cows were swept into the Rhine. No lives were lost, for we had notice of the fall in time; but everything except our lives was gone. When we could venture to the wreck, we stood upon a field of snow. We dug into the heap by chance, for no one knew exactly where his cottage lay. All marks had perished in that common grave. At last we found the church, and then we opened out our trenches right and left. It was a trying task; for as we cut our lanes the sides fell in and blocked us up. But worse was yet in store for us. In spring the snow began to melt by day, and freeze again by night. The surface soon became one sheet of ice. Our hamlet was a glacier, with the drip and rot of ice above whatever of our household stuff had not been crushed and spoiled. When we could count our loss, some restless people said we must remove from Selva, seek a home elsewhere, and leave our grounds as pastures. Nay, they sent to Chur and Bern, and begged for leave to go their ways. For once the Bernese folk were right; they said we must remain at Selva, and the younger men were glad to find it so.'

'Then you rebuilt your houses?'

'Roughly, as you see; but still they serve. The wind gets through the slits and cracks, but peasants cannot live in palaces. We raised our little church. We planted on this alp yon hedge of pines, and put up prayers to Mary and the Saints. Since then we have been spared.'

His tale is true, excepting as to why the peasants would not move, and how the planting of the Milez alp was done. So soon as news of that great avalanche came to Bern, an engineer was sent to see the ruins and report upon their cause. That cause was but too clear; the rustics had been cutting down the pines, each woodman for himself, until the screen of forest was too weak to hold the weight of snow. The Federal Council put no veto on the plan for settling in another place; the Council had no power to stop them if they wished to go; but, like so many Communes in these Celtic alps, they came with cap in hand for money, and the Federal Council could not satisfy their greed. When they had brought this ruin on their fields, they asked the Government to turn their losses into gains. To go elsewhere they wanted such and such round sums. The Commune said it was too poor to move; the Canton that it was too poor to help. An engineer, who came from Bern to look at the affair, reported that the Federal Council might contribute so and so. The Selvians would not take so small a gift; they built their houses frailer than before; and then the Federal Council planted this new pine-wood on the Milez alp. Since then the village has been safe; and every Selvian thinks he owes that safety to his saints.

Below us, in the Rhone valley, on the road from Oberwald to Ulrichen, stands the thorpe of Obergestelen, which has suffered more than Selva in the upper Rhine. The place has often been destroyed by snow-slides, storms of rain, and atmospheric fires. Two days ago a peasant pointed out to me a grave in which are laid the ashes of eighty-four persons, male and female, killed by one avalanche in a single night. Three years ago, this village was consumed by fire. It was a hot September afternoon; the men were on the mountains with their herds; some women and the children only were at home. A sultry mist lay on the thorpe, from which a cloud of smoke was seen to rise. The herdsmen hurried down the slopes; but now a hot wind rose and drove the flames across the narrow streets. In two hours all was over. Out of sixty-eight houses and a hundred and twelve out-buildings only three were saved. The church was charred and rent; the sheds in which the peasants dwelt were cinders; and the village streets and gardens made a desert. Hardly any one had a roof-tree under which to lay his head. Some wandered wildly to and fro. One body went to Ulrichen, a second marched on Oberwald. These sought relief at Rekingen, and those at Goschinen and Münster. Others threw themselves among the ruins of their homes; and two poor creatures sat them down in their dismay and died.

Yet Obergestelen is rebuilt once more. And not as Selva is rebuilt—a little frailer than before. She is rebuilt of rock. A man of science came to see the wreck; his science told him that her only safety lay in stone; and Obergestelen, now laid out in streets, with houses built of stone, is free in future from all fear of fire.

'Teutonic,' nods the Engineer; 'Obergestelen

is Teutonic—Selva is Romonsch;' and having given this hint, he smiles, as though the last word on that subject has been said.

'Ave Maria!' sighs the Nun.

CHAPTER V.

RAIN AND ROCKS.

A FLOOD of rain may try men's natures on these heights more sternly than a slide of snow, and even than an atmospheric fire. An avalanche, a conflagration, overwhelms a single thorpe; such floods of rain as drench these central alps may sweep a hundred miles of valley bare of house and tree.

One night, three years ago, a few days after the great fire which lapped up Obergestelen, the gates of heaven were opened on this mountain ridge. It was a Sunday night. The day had been of sultry warmth, and all the summer had been strangely hot. No snow lay near the Furka. Slopes that commonly retain their whiteness through the year were brown and bare. The Siedeln glacier shrank behind the Furka horn; the foot of the Rhone glacier was a shoal of earth and sand; in all the lateral gulleys there were becks and falls; and never, in the memory of men, had such a melting of the permanent ice been known. Not once, but many times, the Rhone had broken through her dykes. The Reuss, the Rhine, and the Ticino had been swollen, and dams constructed in these rivers had been loosened in a hundred joints. At length the clouds discharged their burden on the earth.

A flash — a roll of thunder — and the rain came pattering on the rocks. Descending from the Furka, from the Thierberg, from the Tiefen glacier, the waters leapt into the road at Re Alp, drowned the fields at Hospenthal, destroyed the roads and water-works at Andermatt, and, gathering fury as they roared past Teufelstein, smote the strong town of Amstäg, where the Kastelen drops into the Reuss. A blow, the dyke gave way. The waters surged into the garden, sucked through walls, and washed out herbs and fruit-trees with the soil in which they grew. A house began to float. The inmates cried for help; but night and storm were round them, with a roar of falling rain, of hurrying floods, of crashing forests, and of parting roofs; and as the timbers strained the roof fell in. A second and a third house followed, and the beams, dashed downwards, added to the wreck. At Silinen the waste was wide and stern; the town was all but washed away; roads, bridges, farmsteads, gardens, all went madly down into the lake. This hamlet was the greatest sufferer from that fall of rain; her loss being reckoned by the Federal engineers at a hundred and twenty thousand francs; but Erstfeld, lower down the stream, a poorer place, and one in which the land is tilled by peasant owners, had a deeper part in the despair. A hundred rustics lost their all that night.

A dozen lateral valleys of the Reuss bring torrents to the lake—the Evi, Tief, and Schächen, for example,—all of which fell into and inflamed the flood. Near Attinghausen stronger dams were built. Few rivers in the world can match the Reuss in fall; in thirty miles this river drops five thousand feet. A deluge, therefore, may be always coming; and the river-banks at Attinghausen, Altdorf, Seedorf, and Flüelen have been strongly dammed. On Sunday night the floods were stronger than these powerful works. A breach was made at Attinghausen in the dyke; a second breach soon followed, and the waters ran out screaming through the fields. At evening, ere the storm began, the lake was very low; a long, hot summer having sucked it up to an unusual depth; but when the daylight came the churchyard and the inns were all below the water lines.

In Canton Uri only, five hundred persons lost a great part of their worldly wealth; and even the Federal engineers computed that the cost of that one night of rain, in this short Uri valley, was about five hundred thousand francs.

But cruel as the ravage was in Canton Uri, it was greater in the Valais and Graubünden. In Ticino it was worst of all.

Val Blegno, in Ticino, is a mountain passage of peculiar beauty. Nestling in between the peaks and crests of Scopi and La Bianca, where the roads are very steep, the cascades spring from ledge to ledge amidst a crowd of pretty modern châlets and the ruins of an ancient world. For here and there, among the vineyards and the chestnut-groves, you come upon some Romanesque tower. As usual with a Latin people every perch of ground belonging to the rustic has been turned to use as either garden, paddock, or plantation; and as usual also with a Latin people every patch of wood belonging to the Commune has been cut away. Few hollows in this chain of alps can show more contrasts than the Blegno. Vines are grown on frames, and melons in the courtyards; chestnut-trees and walnut-trees abound, the fruit of which the peasants roast and vend; but high above the nooks in which these fruit-trees thrive, with garden, church, and house, is seen a mass of rock, a thousand feet in height, without a bush from base to crown, although the heights above are capped with meadows of unmelting snow.

For many weeks before that Sunday night, while it was hot and dry at Chur and Brieg, much rain was falling in the Blegno, and the water-ways were greatly worn and torn. Then came the night, when shepherds who were sleeping in the mountains, say, that rain fell, not in showers but sheets, and that the solid earth was shaken by the weight. All valleys on the slopes of the St. Gothard were invaded by the floods. From seven to ten o'clock the storm increased in noise and fury. As the lightning flashed and thunder broke, enormous streams of water rolled down every rift and scoop. The Campo and the Compietto were two roaring torrents. Camha was a cataract. From Olivione to Bianca nearly all the dams gave way; the bed, so deep before, was raised by the accumulating sand and stones, till meadow lands which lay on either bank were swept. At Aquarosso, Dongio, and Polleggio, lands, and trees, and soil were carried off like so much dust. Whatever stood in front of that descending rush, as dykes, walls, bridges, houses, mills, and stables, fell into the stream. In many parts the waters left their usual beds and leapt by garden walls and private paths into the hamlets, filled the cowsheds and the dairies, underflowed the beams, and lifted the strong habitations off the earth. Enormous slabs of rock were hurled into the valleys, and an engineer from Zürich found one fragment of a thousand cubic feet.

The feature of that fearful night in Blegno was descending slips of earth and rock. In Val Soglia, all the tracks were covered by these falling masses. In Semiona and Malvaglia, several persons lost their lives. One hamlet, that of Cumiasca, was a tragic scene. Some fifteen houses occupied a grassy slope, from which the rustics had completely stript the pines. That Sunday night these rustics went to bed, as alpine rustics do, at sun-down; but were soon awakened by the elemental war. They are not very brave, at best, these Cumiasca Celts; and roused at dead of night, in utter darkness, in the midst of drenching rain, and with a roar of falling stones about their ears, they rushed into the open road, took counsel of each other's fears, and turned their faces to the mountain wall. Great blocks of stone were tumbling from the skies. Some fugitives were struck and killed. Some lost their senses, and returned to what had been their homes; the rest roamed madly up and down the gorge all night. In all some twenty persons lost their lives.

When morning came, the few who had survived their fellows tried to find their houses. Not a shed was standing in its place. They looked upon the wreck, and thought it must be all a dream. How could a single night have stript them so? A heap of earth and stones lay over what had yesterday been Cumiasca. Full a quarter of the villagers were dead, and nearly half of those who had not perished in the night were crazed. What could they do in face of such a trial? Each one looked into his neighbour's face for hope, and found no comfort. In a body they sat down upon the earth and wept.

The engineers who came from Bern to help them, were astonished by their broken spirit, as a worse calamity than even the destruction of their homes. The men were patient in their misery; supporting loss of food and fuel with a resignation truly southern; but they could not front the facts and rise to overcome them at a bound. In turns they moped, and cursed, and cried. They threw themselves before their saints. They told the engineer they had no hope, and could not make an effort to begin the world afresh. Some houses, only partly covered by the rubbish, could be recognised; but not a man in Cumiasca had the heart to clear them out. Yet men and women were gentle in their ways. No begging was perceived, and every one seemed pleased with what was given him from the common fund.

It was the same elsewhere on the Italian side. The League came in with work, as well as money. All the roads were injured; some of them were stopped. The people of whole villages were called upon to clear these paths—men, women, children —every one who could raise a pick and move a stone. The men were armed with spade and axe; the women carried lengths of rope; and while these men were levelling the road behind in single files, some thirty women moved in front of them and tugged the greater fragments to one side. The little ones were made to pick up stones, according to their strength. Soon every one was got to work once more, and with returning labour came the courage to confront their altered lot.

'These trials,' says the man of Science, who was in Ticino in that day of trouble, 'are a legacy from those saints.'

The Nun lifts up her eyes.

'These fellows dream and dawdle when they ought to stand about their guns; supposing, if they only shut their eyes and gape, that San Gennaro and San Carlo will protect their sheds and fields. They will cut down their woods, and will not dam their streams. We came one day into Polleggio, which had suffered from the floods. . . .'

'But not so much as she deserved,' cries Sister Agnes, with a flush of Celtic fire in her moist eyes. 'Of all the sins in this bad Canton of Ticino, that of Polleggio is the worst. Some hamlets only drive away one priest; Polleggio drives away from her a school of priests. You say the saints have sent these chastisements of storm and rain. You may be right, though in a better sense; for Heaven, though it may suffer long, must overtake the guilty ones at last.'

'Your Church affairs are not my study,' says the Engineer; 'but still one knows that in the general rising of Ticino, not against their bishop only, but against the Holy See as his abettor, these rustics of Polleggio have not borne a leading part. The seminary for priests, established in their neighbourhood, was closed by public acts.'

'It is the same to God,' exclaims the Nun.

'Are you aware,' the man of Science turns to me and asks, 'how much this folly of the rustic Communes costs the League? A hundred thousand francs a-year for cones and shoots. Last year we voted fifty thousand from a special fund. These francs are spent in planting trees; and from my studies of the forests I can say the money is not much. Ten million francs are needed to restore the forests on these central alps alone; six millions more should be expended on the minor alps. Nor is the money all our charge. These Communes draw upon our time, our patience, and our science. If we left these Celtic clowns to chop and burn another twenty years, our hills would be as bare as those of Greece.'

'Can you prevent this waste by Federal law?'

'Not yet: in six months we shall have the power. Such woods are Communal woods. A Commune is a small republic, with indefinite rights; and as the Cantons shrink from trenching on the Communal ground, Bern only can provide a cure. Already we have made one step. In granting aid to sufferers from the recent floods we bound the villagers to whom we paid our money to replant their woods. Our next step is to strip them of their power to fell and burn. Such people are not fit for freedom. To be free, a man must first be master of himself; and these poor things would burn a larch to roast a pan of nuts. All mountain forests will be brought within the scope of Federal law. These rustics must be startled from their sleep. An officer from Bern will soon be at their doors, to let them know that if they choose to roast their nuts with pine and larch they must not drown the lands of people in the vales. We shall protect these folks against their saints.'

'Adieu!' says Sister Agnes, rising from her bench, her cheek aghast with fear and rage.

'Adieu!' the Bernese laughs, with his cold, careful eyes upon her, and the mallet in his upraised hand, as though in such a cause he was prepared to smite the rock of Rome.

'Adieu!' I add, 'but we shall meet again.'

'At Meinrad's Cell in Canton Schwyz?'

'Yes; at the Festival of the Rosary. Adieu! I shall be there, and count the pilgrims at Our Lady's shrine.'

CHAPTER VI.

TEUTON AND CELT.

'A TEUTON finds his Celtic neighbour hard to take?'

'It is so,' says the Bernese; 'but we know our man, and how to deal with him. It is a kind of game. You have to use him well — a little more in word than fact — and then to wait his mood, with now and then a hint, thrown out as though it were by chance, that he is weak while you are strong, that he is naked and adoze while you are armed and on the watch. He has his noble flights, our Celtic friend; and, like poor Sister Agnes, he can fling himself away. We must indulge him, for we want an outpost at our enemy's lines. Two Celtic nations, France and Italy, are the foes we dread; and it is well for us to have a sweep of country in our front, from Basel to Lugano, occupied by Celts. But how are we to keep these borders free? In one of two ways only: we may keep them by the strong hand, we may keep them by the just hand. We have tried both systems, and have found the cost of justice less than that of force. Not long ago Teutonic Switzerland was lord of all the rest. Bern ruled in Canton Vaud; Geneva was her vassal. Upper Valais, peopled by the Teuton, ruled in Lower Valais, peopled by the Celt. Val Leventina and the circles of Lugano and Bellinzona were but conquered provinces of the League. Neufchatel found her centre of political life in Bern. But in revenge of nature, we, the old free citizens of Bern, became the vassals of some noble houses, which had gained hereditary power as officers and satraps in our subject states. What should we gain by putting out our strength once more? Our Celtic brethren would protest. Suppose we answer that the law is with majorities? They fly to arms; we crush them; but our League of freemen dies a violent death. Our actual state is better than such triumph. We must take the evil and the good together, even though we fret against the separate Cantonal vote, and fume most sorely at the Communal local life.'

In mere extent of surface Celtic Switzerland is nearly equal to Teutonic Switzerland; but when we count the people there are only thirty Celts to every seventy Teutons; and the thirty Celts are scattered into three distinct and hostile camps. One camp is Gallic, one Romonsch, and one Italian.

'We come into these hills to-day,' observes the Teuton, 'as our fathers came a thousand years ago; we come from Lombardy, from Swabia, and from Burgundy; we meet on these high crests—around the Ober Alp, the Furka, and the Sasso di Gottardo—and we try to push each other down the slope. We Teutons bear our language to the summit of each pass. The Celts, too, bring their language to the summit of each pass. Our language is High German in the colleges, Low German in the streets. Their language is of more variety than ours. We speak the Allemannic idiom mainly, as our kinsmen speak it in the Rhineland, from the quays of Rorschah to the gates of Metz. They speak three several forms of Latin—French, Italian, and Romonsch; French in the Rhone system, Italian in the Po system, Romonsch in the Inn system, and in the upper portion of the Rhine.

The Federal Hall in Bern has a department of

Statistics, where one of the most learned statists of our time, Max Wirth, sits brooding over lists; for counting people and arranging facts is an essential function of the state; and Wirth is said to know not only every goat and cow, but every tree and almost every blade of grass, in Switzerland. Some mornings spent in this department of Statistics has enriched me with a world of useful facts.

The Switzers were enumerated, they and their belongings, on the first day of December last. Not many strangers are in Switzerland so late, and of the strangers who are noted in the lists as such (in number, 13,852), the greater part are living in the land. The totals are:—

Population in December, 1870.

Males	1,305,670
Females	1,364,675
Total	2,670,345

Excess of females over males, 59,005.

This excess of female life is rather more than in surrounding countries, and is not explained by what is held to be the cause of our disparities of sex in England—emigration of the single men. A second schedule gives us these results:—

Number of Families . . . 557,820
Number of Houses 390,318

The families are small for countries which are mainly tenanted by a Teutonic race.

Two points are to be noted in these figures; first, the number of persons in each Family; and next, the great excess of Families over Houses. On the average for all Switzerland, a Family consists of less than five members: father, mother, and three children; while the average of other countries of Teutonic race is six and seven. The village system, as in Russia, tends to check the natural rate of growth. In counting roofs, we find the number of Families in great excess of Houses; very near a third part of the whole.

Excess of Families over Houses . . 167,502

The village system, as in Russia, tends to check the growth of separate roof-trees.

The number of households is in large excess of the number of houses in which they have to live. Every third family must dwell beneath a roof-tree not its own.

In Languages we find:

Families speaking	German	. . .	384,561
,,	,, French	. . .	134,183
,,	,, Italian	. . .	30,293
,,	,, Romonsch	. . .	8,759
,,	,, English	. . .	19
,,	,, Dutch, Polish, Magyar, Russ, and Spanish (one each)	.	5
		Families	557,820

The first four groups are native, and require to have their separate books of law. It would be something if each idiom had a Canton or a group of Cantons to itself; but such is not the rule, and hardly the exception to a rule. In each of the twenty-five Cantons and Half-cantons you hear German spoken, but in none of these exclusively. In nineteen Cantons and Half-cantons you hear French; in some but little, and in others much, but not in one exclusively. In twenty-one Cantons and Half-cantons there is some Italian, if not much; but no one Canton speaks Italian exclusively. The Romonsch idiom is less widely spread, yet Romonsch may be heard in twelve several Cantons as a native speech. There are, of course, some zig-zag and concentric lines of language. German, which is heard in every Canton of the Bund, maintains a large predominance in Zürich, Bern, Luzern, and all the upper Cantons, with the one exception of Graubünden. French is the prevailing tongue in Neufchatel, Geneva, Valais, Vaud, and Fribourg; but in Vaud and Fribourg German is the language of a strong minority of the people—close upon a third. Italian has its chief seats in Graubünden and Ticino; in the first of which Cantons nearly nine thousand families speak Romonsch. This Rustic Latin is the only language in the country which is dying out. Italian, French, and German grow with the growth of population more or less. The increase in the last ten years stands thus:—

Increase in the number of families speaking—
Italian	1,596
French	10,745
German	17,496

Romonsch is failing; giving way to German, which is taught in every public school. In 1860 there were 8882 families in the country speaking Romonsch; in 1870 there were 8759. Graubünden is the modern Babel. In this mountain Canton dwell some twenty thousand families speaking as returned below:—

Speaking German	9328 families.
,, Romonsch	8715
,, Italian	3000
,, French	29

The differences of race are mostly those of language, but not always. In the twenty-five Cantons and Half-cantons there are :—

Of Teutonic race . . .	2,000,000 souls.
Of Celtic race . . .	670,000

The two great races hold their natural lines; the Northern races nearly all the north, the Southern races nearly all the south. But two exceptions to the law are visible,—one exception in the Rhone valley; a second exception in the Rhine valley. Up to Sion the Rhone is Celtic; at Sierre it is mixed; and higher up the stream is wholly Teutonic. Up to Chur the Rhine is German, but in Ilanz it is mixed, and higher up the stream is Romonsch. What cause has brought this contradiction to a natural law? The structure of these mountain walls. The valley of the Rhone is long and narrow. France has but one opening into it beyond the passage at Villeneuve,—the high and lateral entry from Chamounix by the Forclaz. Only through these gorges can the Gauls from Burgundy and Savoy pour into the Valais; but in passing up the river, they are met in front, and taken on the flank, by Teutons coming by the Furka pass from Andermatt, the Grimsel pass from Meyringen, the Gemmi pass from Unterseen, the Col du Rawyl from Thun, the Sanetsch pass from Gsteig and Saanen. Met by these descending masses, they retire on Sion, where they hold their ground, and keep the forms of Latin life. Five passes through their mountains make the Teutons masters of the Upper Rhone. But Nature, which has given the Teuton access to his neighbour's river, has denied him access to his own. From Ober Alp to Trons, in the Fore Rhine valley, there is not a chamois trail across the northern heights. From Trons and Flims there rise two bridle paths; near Ilanz is an opening to the Panix; but these paths are high and hard to climb; while on the southern bank a dozen easy roads lead in and out of the Italian valleys; roads from Albula, from Stalla from Splügen, from Bernardina, from Olivone, from Val Piora and from Airolo. Thus, a counter march to what has given the upper waters of the Rhone to men of northern race, has given the upper waters of the Rhine to men of southern race. A Teutonic colony has pushed towards Italy; and if they have not crossed the ridge, these colonists hold the mountains to the top. They own the hamlets of the Rheinwald and the pastures of Averserthal. Some German thorpes are circled by a foreign population, like the German colonies in Russia. One such thorpe is that of Bosco, in Ticino. St. Martin and Obersaxen are Teutonic thorpes.

'You see,' the Bernese adds, as we go over all these curious facts, 'we are an odd amalgam of all races and all creeds. We speak Italian, Romonsch, French, and German. We are Lutheran, Calvinist, Catholic, Israelite. We are Latin, Gallic, Low Dutch, High Dutch, Hebrew. We are not a nation, even as we are not a people. We have Communes, Cantons, and Half-cantons, but as yet we have no Switzerland. A Switzer has his Commune, but he has no country. You will hear in Bern that we are twenty-five republics, but in truth we are five hundred republics; every one of these republics with a local life and independent claims. Our Communes were republics once, and have not wholly lost their sovereign rights.'

CHAPTER VII.

THE COMMUNES.

WHEN Bourbaki, rapidly recoiling from the gates of Belfort and the guns of Manteufel, tumbled over into Canton Neufchâtel, the Swiss Society of Public Usefulness—a rich and patriotic body—snatched the moment (Monday, Feb. 20, 1871) when eighty thousand French troops were scattered far and wide among five hundred Communes — ten in one place, forty in a second, seventy in a third — to give the fugitives some lessons in the art of being free.

These strangers were republicans, but not as Switzers are republicans. The French Republic, under which they served, is One and Indivisible. She sweeps away all barriers, landmarks, and distinctions. She erases history. She hates the names of hamlet, city, province; will not hear of Breton, Nizzard, Gascon; rolls a level over the rough soil of France, and makes one family of the tribes and nations she has gathered to her flag. She has one head, one heart, one hand, in which her thought, her blood, her force, reside. She is impatient of provincial rule, and finds in unity the principle of her life. These strangers knew so little of the Switzers, as to fancy that a French and Swiss republic were the same affair. They dreamt, that on a proclamation at the Hôtel de Ville in Paris, the Jura mountains fell for ever; that in fact, if not as yet in form, the Swiss republic was absorbed by France.

It was regarded as a work of public usefulness to clear their brains of all such notions; to inform these strangers of the actual truths; to show them how a Swiss republic differs from a French.

A little book, a souvenir of Switzerland, was printed by the Bernese press; containing, in the simplest words, a true account of what the Swiss republic is—the Commune, Canton, and Confederation—with the rights which every Switzer holds by birth. A copy of this book was given to every soldier of the French republic quartered in a Swiss hamlet; and it might be well if such a souvenir of Switzerland were given to every stranger coming to the alps. Swiss life is not a simple thing. These villagers and burghers have the art of being free; yet not the art of being free as men in England and America are free. A Swiss republic has more likeness to an American republic than a French; but there are points in which the League of Cantons differs utterly from the United States. Some days ago, a liberal orator, when speaking at Versailles, declared that France desires to have a form of government such as people find at Washington and Bern. How all the journals in this country laughed! 'Are we the same?' they asked in mockery; 'we, who build the whole of our political edifice on the Commune—a foundation utterly unknown in the United States?' The Switzers know their country better; and by this time thousands of Bourbaki's troops are able to instruct the French.

The integer of Swiss political society is not the individual, not the household, but the Commune.

In the passing hour this name of Commune stinks in many nostrils with the reek of powder and petroleum; and in ears disposed to catch at sounds, the very word suggests a dance of death. A fire breaks out in the Rue du Rhone, Geneva.

The wind is very high; the fire brigade is slow; and house by house, the conflagration spreads, until it nears the lake. Vast crowds of people fill the streets; the civic guards turn out; the councillors of state are on the ground; and in the noise of shouting crowds, and falling roofs, and roaring winds, the flames are mastered and repressed. Next day, an article appears in the Paris *Gaulois*, dated from Geneva, hinting that this fire is not an accident, that agents are employed, and that Geneva will be burnt as Paris has been burnt. This evidence is given. A person in the crowd, his name not known, is heard to cry, 'Burn the aristocrats — Long live the Commune!' Being seized by well-dressed people, he is shielded by a mob of working men, and gets away unhurt. At once the *Journal de Genève* replies that no such scene occurred. Jules Klein, the correspondent of the *Gaulois*, answers that he heard the words and saw the man arrested and released. The words were Vive la Commune! Klein is justified by facts. Then comes the culprit with his word; he is a Genevese, one Etienne Perrudet, who ran to help the firemen, and assisted at the pumps from midnight until dawn. On leaving off, he meets some firemen from Boäge, a village near Geneva, whom he greets with cries of Vive la Commune de Boäge! Some persons, hearing only half his greeting, lay their hands on him, but when the firemen tell these persons what has passed, they break into a laugh and send him to his breakfast with a merry shout!

But though the Commune smells just now of fire and ashes, yet the thing itself is old, and almost sacred; for the Commune is a part of our most ancient record, part of our Bible history and of our human life. In Oriental countries it is still familiar to men's eyes and thoughts; and if our western world is leaving it behind—as finding no more use for it—the Commune still exists as a political and social form, in every country of the rising sun, from Russia, Palestine, and Egypt, to the farther kingdoms of the East.

In the United States, they take the individual man as unit, and all public franchises are vested in that individual man. The individual votes. In England we are apt to treat the household as the unit, and to vest the franchise in the house. With us the roof-tree votes. In Russia they regard the individual and the family as fractions of the Commune. There the Commune votes, pays taxes, fills the ranks, divides the soil, and exercises magisterial power. In Switzerland the Commune has an almost equal rank. A Commune has its own estate; the land on which the people who compose it live. In olden times, this land was held in common, as such land is held in Russia now; but much of it has passed from public custody into private hands. Yet every Commune owns some land, some wood, some water-right, in common fee. These riches are the Communal fund, in which each member of the Commune has an equal share.

Some thinkers of the highest class contend that this Swiss village system is a great success. 'Observe my country,' says a voice, to which one cannot choose but listen; 'what is there to see? Free speech, free roads, free trade. You meet no soldiers in our streets. You are not troubled by police. We have no village parson, and no country squire. Our towns are orderly, our hamlets clean. Our schools, our mills, our forests, are alive with people, every child and every man of whom is as a lord unto himself. This order of our people has the order of our Communes for its natural source.' The Swiss Society of Public Usefulness declare, in the souvenir given to Bourbaki's troops, 'Our laws proceed from this great principle, that our institutions are truly free and popular only in so far as our Communes are free.' The Commissioners appointed by the National Council to revise the Federal constitution say, in their report (May 5, 1871), 'The liberty of the Swiss Commune is justly considered as the school and cradle of our political liberties.'

Swiss Communes are not modelled, like the Russian Communes, on a single type. In Canton Geneva there are forty-four Communes; in Graubünden there are two hundred and five Communes. In fact, these Communes differ very much in size, in form, in wealth, in rules. In some Cantons they are open; but in many Cantons they are closed. In some the craft and calling of a member is a capital point. In others, birth is prized; not blood, as in a country ruled by nobles, but a birth-right in the soil—a preference given to Bernese Teuton over Swabian Teuton, to a Valaisian Celt over a Savoyard Celt. In some religion is a test. Some Communes claim no higher powers than may be exercised in England by a trading company—a bank, a railway, or a joint-stock farm. Such easy bodies may be found by hundreds in the richer and more prosperous Cantons, Zürich, Aargau, Vaud, and Bern. But many of the Communes claim the rights of independent states — a right to cut down trees, to injure dykes, and open gaming-houses at the public cost. Such difficult bodies may be found in plenty in the poorer and more ignorant Cantons, Valais, Appenzel, Graubünden, and Ticino.

Yet, in these varieties, there is a common life. Each Commune is a small republic, with her free and equal members, her assemblies, ballots, and debates, her mayor and council, and her Communal lists.

A Communal Assembly is the whole body of members properly convened in either market, public-house, or open field; where they can make their by-laws, and elect a council and a mayor. These officers must be chosen from the list of citizens who have a right to vote. As women have no votes, they are not called upon to serve. In every village, lists are kept, and every member has his name inscribed. Inscription is his proof of citizenship. Each member has the same rights as every other member. No precedence is allowed. In Switzerland there may be families as old as any in the empires on her borders. Not a little of the proudest blood in Europe flows from castles on these alps. The Austrian Kaisers come from Habsburg, in the Canton Aargau; and the German Kaisers draw their line from Neufchatel. But the oldest families are like the newest; they must stand on living merit, not on long descent. No thought is given to birth. All families, a Switzer holds, are of an equal age and equal rank.

These citizens, who may be woodmen, goatherds, weavers, what not, name the mayor and council of the Commune from their body, and the officers thus selected are the sole authorities in the place. They must be five—a mayor and four citizens; in larger villages they may be ten. Much work falls on them, which they cannot shirk. They serve two years at least, and may be kept in office six. No man is free to either serve or not as suits his mood; the Commune must be served. A man selected by his equals takes his spell of office, as he takes in earlier days his spell of school, and in his later day his spell of camp.

CHAPTER VIII.

COMMUNAL AUTHORITIES.

THE cares which fall upon these village rulers are of many kinds.

A mayor and council are the fathers of the Commune; nothing can be done without their leave. In countries where the Commune is unknown, in which the mayor and council are replaced by squire and curate, every one is free to act as he thinks well, and eat the fruit of what he plants; but in a Commune, men are guided by the mayor. A school-boy who has been expelled for sloth or surliness can only be admitted to his class again by intervention of his mayor. A goatherd who has fallen in love with village maiden, cannot wed his lass without permission from his mayor.

These peasant magistrates have charge of the estate. They watch the roads and streets, they keep the fountains running, they observe who comes and goes each day, they guard the fields from torrents and the sheds from fire, they see that children walk straight home from school, they send on tramps, and write and keep the communal lists. They make and execute the local rules. They say which pines are to be cut, which roads must be repaired, which torrents should be bridged. They hold the poor fund and drive away such persons as they find unprofitable members of their guild.

The poor have claims, not only on the lands and forests held in common, but on certain funds which have been set apart as poor funds, and on all the charities of a Christian land. A Commune may be very poor—some Communes in Graubünden and the Valais say they are extremely poor—but even in Graubünden and the Valais there is nothing like a settled pauper class. These Communes will not let a pauper class grow up. A sot, a sluggard, and a fool, must tramp. They have no room for such a man, nor can he skulk into a hole and live upon their earnings like a rat. They smoke him out; they take him to the village mayor; they tell him he must try some other place. They hint that either France, or Austria, or America, would be his field. If he is slow to see their drift, they help him with a few plain words. At last he sees that he must trudge, and then they pay his fare to Paris, to Vienna, to New York. This fare may be a hundred francs, three hundred francs, five hundred francs; but down it goes upon the nail; the wastrel packs his trap; the Commune shakes him off for good and bad.

The mayor and council have to build the primary schools, to seek the teachers, to inspect the class-rooms, to enforce the rules and regulations, to prevent disorder, to preside at festivals and promotions, to instruct the careless parent in his duties, to supply the means, both moral and material, for attaining and preserving the highest character for their village schools.

A man of any craft and creed may claim to have his part in any Commune where he dwells; but then this Commune is the judge of whether she will grant his prayer or not. She can refuse his claim and give no reason why. Before she listens to his suit at all, she asks him for a proof of his nationality, a certificate of his good life and manners, evidence of his ability to support himself and his belongings, testimony that he has not lost his civic rights by condemnation in a court of law. Such proofs are scanned with jealous eyes. Though nothing may be found against the man, his suit may be rejected by the village sires. In any case there will be money to pay down; but money is not all in all. Paternal governors are hard to please. They may not like his looks; they may dislike his creed. A dwarf, a cretin, or a cripple, would be turned adrift by any communal mayor without a word. In many parts religion is the primary test. Among the nimble, jealous, and artistic folks of Neufchâtel and Vaud, engaged in making clocks, a Jew would have no chance. Among the stolid, picturesque, and hardy folk of Appenzel-inner-Rhoden, tending kine and making cheese, a Lutheran would have no chance. A right of settling where he likes, of changing his abode from year to year, and striking root in any mountain side, is not a right to which the Switzer, free as he may call himself, is born.

This name of Switzer, borne so proudly in all foreign countries by the men who own it, has a meaning for the stranger which it hardly bears at home. A man of English blood first thinks of himself as being an Englishman, then as being a Londoner, and only in the third degree as being a Paddingtonian. A man of Swiss descent reverses this arrangement. He is first (say) a Wiesbacher, then a Bernese, afterwards a Switzer. He is conscious of an overmastering law. 'We move,' explains the Swiss Society of Public Usefulness in their souvenir, 'from low to high; the Commune is the centre of our life; and there can be no true development of liberty except so far as it proceeds from the Commune —from the centre to the circling lines.'

A Switzer's right of settlement on his native soil, though urged in many quarters, is not popular in any Commune. Five or six attempts to get the Cantons to adopt the general principle that a Switzer has a right to settle where he pleases in the territories of the League have failed: the last attempt so lately as five years ago. The leading Cantons—Zürich, Bern, Luzern, Geneva—press the doctrine; but the smaller Cantons, Uri, Valais, Schwyz, and the two Half-cantons of Unterwalden, will not yield. Appenzel-inner-Rhoden will admit a Catholic to her Communes, but she shuts her gates on every Lutheran and on every Jew.

A Commune is in part a guild, with common property in trust; in part a congregation, with a common faith in charge; and the religious question weighs with some far more than any thought of worldly goods. In every case the entry of a stranger is regarded as a privilege— the only privilege existing in this pure democracy —and, like all privilege, is an affair of sale. Some Communes have a tariff, which is fixed by the assembly, and deposited with the mayor; a tariff raised or lowered according to the market in such things.

In Communes like Lausanne and Bern, which own large tracts of land and forest, prices may be high; from fifty to a thousand francs, according to the age and sex, the country and condition, of the stranger coming in. A boy pays more than a girl; a married man pays more than a single man; a foreigner pays more than a native. In the Commune of Lausanne, the tariff has been lowered this autumn; not without a serious fight in favour of the Commune as against the citizen. In older times, the Communes of Lausanne regarded Bernese, Zürichers, and other Switzers, in the light of strangers, and the charge for their admission was the same as for admitting Russians, French, and Danes. It was suggested by M. Pidon, one of the commissioners of revision, that the privilege of a lower price enjoyed by citizens of Canton Vaud should be extended to all citizens of the Swiss League. At first his views were hooted down, as tending towards a red republic; for in Canton Vaud, a Commune is the stronghold of conservative opinions; but a patriotic spirit was created by the recent war which gave M. Pidon unexpected strength. He placed the Swiss Idea under vivid lights; and in the end his motion was adopted by the Council. Friday, Nov. 3, 1871, was a great day in the Commune of Lausanne; for on that day a Bernese and a Züricher were accepted by the Vaudois capital as something nearer than a Russian and a Dane.

The tariff of the Commune of Lausanne now stands :—

For Vaudois and other Switzers.

Head of a Family	500 francs.
A Married Son	350 ,,
An Unmarried Son	150 ,,
A Daughter	75 ,,

A double rate is fixed for foreigners :—

For Non-Switzers.

Head of a Family	1000 francs.
A Married Son	700 ,,
An Unmarried Son	300 ,,
A Daughter	150 ,,

The open fine on marriage is not the least curious item in these lists. A married man pays seven hundred francs for self and wife. An unmarried man pays three hundred francs; an unmarried woman pays a hundred and fifty francs. A bachelor and spinster pay together four hundred and fifty francs against seven hundred paid by a wedded pair.

CHAPTER IX.

COMMUNAL GOVERNMENT.

THIS fine imposed on married couples coming into any Commune is no whimsy of a village mayor and council, but the offspring of a settled policy in all the Communes for checking a too rapid growth. A married couple may have children; children mean more mouths to feed; and, in the failure of parental care, these mouths may come upon the Communal funds. So married couples are not wanted in the Communes; if they seek to enter they must pay an extra fine. A guild with property in common has an obvious interest in diminishing the claims upon that property. The natural enemies of such a guild are married people, who may bring new mouths into the world; and therefore married people are discouraged from applying for admission to the Communal mayor.

A cold and jealous eye is bent on any one

within the Commune who may hint that he would like to marry. Every obstacle is raised that can be raised. In many Cantons a man can only marry on the license of his mayor, who may decline to grant such license when circumstances offer him a fair excuse. The man may be too young or he may be too old. He may be halt or blind; he may be deaf or dumb. He may be crazed in mind; and some old bachelor mayor may think the wish to marry very good evidence of craze. He may be poor. The girl he seeks may not be of his Canton. He may have a dubious character in his village. Any reason will suffice. A case is now before the Federal Council on petition. Aloïs Arnold is a peasant, living in his Commune of Attinghausen, in the Reuss valley, near to Altdorf, in the land of William Tell. Six years ago this peasant fell in love with Geneviève Guebey of Onnion, a hamlet in Savoy. Having gained the girl's assent, he claimed a license from his mayor to marry her. The mayor was not in mood. He put the peasant off from time to time; he raised objections more or less insulting; and when pressed to go into the detail and decide upon the license, said he would not move a finger till the girl had paid into his hands a sum of five hundred and seventy-three francs. Then Aloïs took the law upon himself. Retiring for a while from Attinghausen and the land of Tell, he went to live in Savoy, near his promised bride, and married her at Onnion, where the priest made no inquiry for a license from his mayor. Aloïs was merry in his new abode; but Savoy is not Uri; and at length his heart began to yearn for his old garden on the Reuss. He came, he showed his marriage lines, he took his wife to mass; but no one in the hamlet would receive her as an honest woman, or admit his children to their rights of birth. He waited on the mayor; he offered to pay down all fines inflicted by the Cantonal laws on an Uranian who may take a stranger for his wife. The mayor repelled him. Then he went to Altdorf, where the Cantonal Council was in session; but the Cantonal Council would not interfere. Such questions come up every day; in every Commune there is some unhappy Geneviève; and if they meddled in the fray at Attinghausen, they must vex their souls with every wandering shepherd's love affairs. Then Aloïs came to Bern, and threw his story into the great group of facts suggesting a revision of the Federal law.

Another case. A friend of mine is waiting for a train at Biel. A crowd of peasants from the Commune of Diesbach, in the neighbourhood of Büren, come upon the platform, shouting, shivering, sobbing, like a mob of girls. A young man and his bride are with them, who are also crying; for the pair are starting on a journey to the western world—a journey not of their own seeking, but imposed on them by a paternal mayor; and these poor countrymen, in pity for their exile, come to see them off. Paternal government in Diesbach, where the man was born, dislikes to see him marry, for the wretch is suffering from an epileptic fit; and village fathers feel that he and his may be a burthen to their Commune at some future day. The bride, too, has her miseries of the Commune; she belongs to Brügg, and Brügg is tired of her, for she is poor, and has an infant three years old. The mother and her child were found one morning sleeping on a bank, with some small articles in a bag for sale. What could a fatherly mayor suggest, except that they should seek their fortunes in some other place? To marry her, and cast her out, together with her infant child and epileptic husband, into space, would cost some hundred francs. The money was paid down, the pair departed, and the peasants, kinder than their lords, have come with them to Biel, where they will start for Paris, on their way to Havre and New York.

'It is a shameful sight,' a citizen of Biel exclaims; 'these Communes sell their children!'

'Never mind all that,' replies the woman; 'buy a box of matches, please!' And then the train rolls out of Biel.

'It is a burning shame,' remarks the citizen of Biel; 'the country must step in; these peasant mayors and councillors have no heart!'

The functions of these village sires are not defined by law. Each Commune in Graubünden claims to be an independent state. Not long ago such villages as Trons, Dissentis, and Ilanz, exercised the power of life and death. It is not long since Andermatt lost her gallows and her right to hang and quarter. In the Valais there are Communes which regard themselves as separate states. One such commune, that of Saxon, sold a few years since the right to keep a public gaming-table for a certain sum. A company, the Cercle des Etrangers, bought some ground, laid out a garden, built a pretty house, with dancing-room and card-room all complete. The gamblers and the courtesans of Europe flocked to Saxon. Saxon found the sin pay very well; and when the world cried out against her for the shame she brought on Switzerland, the mayor and council snapt their fingers at the men of Bern and Zürich. They were acting in their right. Four million francs were spent on Saxon by these strangers; every one was richer for the outlay; and the money that enriched him came from Paris, Moscow, and Madrid, not Bern and Zürich. Why should Bern and Zürich interfere?

As the world elsewhere is closing all such places, agents are about the Valais tempting other Communes by the chink of gold. These agents want a place with mineral springs; a pretty place it should be, and an idle place it must be. They have been to Monthey, in the Val d'Illies, as well as other Communes on the railway lines; but not, as yet, with much success; for public indignation has been roused; and mayors decline to bring the tempest on their roofs. But Saxon keeps her tables open; pleading that if harm is done, it is to strangers, not to her own people;

that if gambling is immoral, there are many industries about a kursaal which an honest man may ply.

The cantonal authorities are slow to move against a Commune in their district; and by law the Canton, not the Confederation, is the actual State.

CHAPTER X.

CANTONS AND HALF-CANTONS.

The Canton is the State.

Few jurists hold with the mayor of Saxon that any part of Swiss sovereignty resides in a Commune. Jurists of all sections, whether Celtic or Teutonic, whether Catholic or Evangelical, whether Conservative or Radical, admit that Swiss sovereignty resides in the Cantons. When the members for these Cantons meet in Bern, with certain forms, and in a single room, they hold this sovereignty in common; but they bring it into Bern, they do not find it here; and when they leave this town they carry it with them to their several homes.

In speaking roundly one would say there are in Switzerland twenty-two Cantons, which are marked officially and in order, thus:—1. Zürich; 2. Bern; 3. Luzern; 4. Uri; 5. Schwyz; 6. Unterwalden; 7. Glarus; 8. Zug; 9. Fribourg; 10. Solothurn; 11. Basel; 12. Schaffhausen; 13. Appenzell; 14. St. Gallen; 15. Graubünden (Romonsch, Grischa—French, Grisons); 16. Aargau; 17. Thurgau; 18. Ticino; 19. Vaud; 20. Valais; 21. Neufchâtel; 22. Geneva. This arrangement, though historical, does not correspond to the historical growth; for Zürich, now the heart and brain of the republic, was very far from being the original founder of the League. That glory lies with Schwyz; here marked as number 5. Schwyz gave her name, her genius, and her flag, to the Alliance. From Schwyz we get the name of Switzer; the connexion of religion with democracy; the pure white cross upon the blood-red field. When Tell was tending kine at Bürglen, on the Uri slopes, there were no Switzers save the men of Schwyz. Tell never called himself a Switzer. Tell was a Uranian, and his Canton Uri. Schwyz had gained in war—for she was ever stout in fight—the flag she lent her allies of the League. Three other Forest Cantons, Uri, Unterwalden, and Luzern, were in the League while Zürich stood outside—a feudal and imperial town. But Zürich was a rich and powerful city, and the moment she adhered to the Alliance she assumed in it the leading part. Bern followed her, and shared her power. Luzern, as chief of the four Forest Cantons, claimed an equal rank. As soon as any Federal Council met, this council sat by turns in either of these capitals—two years in each. But Zürich and Luzern have each given up the claim to rank as capitals; and now the President, the Council, and the two Assemblies, find a permanent seat in Bern.

Three of these twenty-two republics—Basel, Appenzell, and Unterwalden—have been separated into rival halves; each half-republic keeping her own share of sovereign power. Basel is divided into Basel-stadt and Basel-land; Appenzell into Appenzell-outer-Rhoden and Appenzell-inner-Rhoden; Unterwalden into Unterwalden ob-wald and Unterwalden nid-wald.

These nineteen Cantons and six Half-cantons form the Swiss League. Each part is equal to each other part, in spite of variation as to size, to numbers, and to wealth. The differences are very great. According to the census taken on the first day of December, 1870, the

CANTONS AND HALF-CANTONS.

population and the mileage in each Canton and Half-canton stood :—

CANTONS.	POPULATION.	SQUARE MILES.
1. Bern	501,875	2615
2. Zurich	284,477	659
3. Vaud	229,596	1226
4. Aargau	198,731	538
5. St. Gallen	191,039	781
6. Luzern	132,154	480
7. Ticino	119,312	1082
8. Fribourg	110,536	632
9. Valais	97,409	2016
10. Neufchâtel	95,563	308
11. Thurgau	93,260	384
12. Graubünden	92,793	2706
13. Geneva	89,416	110
14. Solothurn	74,636	292
15. Schwyz	47,728	358
16. Schaffhausen	37,650	118
17. Glarus	35,223	265
18. Zug	20,986	91
19. Uri	16,095	418
HALF-CANTONS.		
1. Basel-land	54,051	166
2. Basel-stadt	47,124	15
3. Appenzell-outer-Rhoden	48,765	102
4. Appenzell-inner-Rhoden	11,926	61
5. Unterwalden-ob-wald,	14,437	186
6. Unterwalden-nid-wald,	11,711	112
	2,656,493	15,721

The rending of full Cantons into Half-cantons is the work of party feuds; in one place springing from political causes, in a second from religious strife, and in a third from wrangles about wood and grass.

From 1501, when Canton Basel joined the League, to 1831, the city ruled the country districts; for the town was wealthy, learned, prosperous; a seat of commerce, with a university, a minster, and a bridge across the Rhine. Some families in the town were noble; many families in the Canton kept a feudal state. These families held the reins, and being chiefly Catholic and Conservative, they drove the farmers of the Jura districts into arms. Not once, but many times, the peasantry surrounded Basel; now and then they hung a burgomeister; but the craft and money of the citizens sufficed to save their city. When the storm of 1830 spread from Paris towards the Rhine, these farmers of the Jura rose once more; the Federal troops were called into the Canton; and, in 1833, an Act of Separation was effected, so that in the future Canton Basel was to be divided into two Half-cantons; into Basel-stadt, with Basel for her seat of government; and Basel-land, with Liesthal for her seat of government. Each moiety sends a deputy to Bern; the city a conservative deputy, the country a democratic deputy — armed with half a vote; and as these deputies vote on opposite sides in nearly every question, Canton Basel is in practice disfranchised by her domestic broils.

The Appenzells were parted into sections long ago; so long ago as 1597; and wholly on account of their religious feuds. The fore-alp districts, dropping towards the Lake of Constanz, listened to the great reformers, while the mountain districts, climbing towards Hoch Sentis, clung to their ancestral church. These fore-alp districts were inhabited by weavers of Teutonic race; those mountain-sides were held by shepherds of a mixed descent, in whom the Romonsch blood was rich and red. A fight ensued, which wasted many villages and cost the Canton many lives; but after years of mutual injury, these kites and crows grew weary of their strife. Each side felt sure it could not break the other; as the mountain country was too rugged for the lowlanders to scale and keep; the lowland hamlets were too many and too populous for the mountaineers to force and hold. A line was therefore drawn between the shepherds and the weavers; each consenting to withdraw beyond this line, and afterwards to live in separate camps. The League was asked to sanction this partition; and the names of Appenzell-outer-Rhoden and Appenzell-inner-Rhoden were bestowed on these Half-cantons. Evangelicals were to live in Appenzell-outer-Rhoden, with the hamlet of Trogen for their seat of government. Catholics were to live in Appenzell-inner-Rhoden, with the hamlet of Appenzell for their seat of government. So these two Half-cantons send their deputies to Bern, in which their two half-votes are mostly thrown away, since they are cast into opposing scales.

Unterwalden was divided into sections long before the Reformation, and in fact before the League itself was formed. A forest called the Kernwald cuts this Canton into two unequal parts, the Ob-wald (over-forest) and the Nid-wald (under-forest); and so early as the twelfth century, the herdsmen who were separated by this forest quarrelled, fought for mastery, and, failing to achieve decisive victory on either side, agreed to live in peace, each section with a capital, a code, a government of its own. Unterwalden-ob-wald placed her capital at Sarnen, by the Lake of Sarnen, in the upper valley. Unterwalden-nid-wald placed her capital at Stanz, midway between the western Aa and eastern Aa. When Unterwalden joined the league of Forest Cantons she retained this old division; so that each Half-Canton is represented in the Federal Council by half a vote.

This tendency of Cantons to divide and cross each other is not dead. For years past Fribourg has been threatened with disruption on her western frontier, and the utmost care is needed to preserve the public peace. A people differing as to race and creed, to speech and occupation, have been thrown together in this Canton Fribourg; Celts and Teutons, Protestants and Catholics, engineers and shepherds; each with habits and opinions which the other loathes as so much spume and spawn tossed upward from the burning lake. One portion of the Canton is entirely Gallic, with a population holding liberal views in politics and evangelical views in church affairs. A second portion of the Canton is entirely German, with a population holding ultramontane views in church and state. The town of Morat, on the Lake of Morat, is the liberal centre; while the town of Fribourg, on the Sarine, is the ultramontane centre. In devotion to this party,

Fribourg bears away the bell from Sion and Luzern. She built a palace for the Jesuits. She gives a home to the Society of Pio Nono. She was foremost in the Separate League. She has an ultramontane Council. She lends herself to every movement of the priestly orders. Evangelical flesh and blood can hardly stand such blind devotion to the Church; and hence the enemies of Rome desire to break this Canton into halves: one fraction having Fribourg—which has never raised, they say, an arm for freedom—as her seat of government; the second fraction having Morat—which, they say, is glorified in history—as her seat of government. By such a split the liberal party would obtain a vote in Bern. The new republic would be liberal, Protestant and French; and Catholic Fribourg's vote would be destroyed by the Protestant Morat's vote.

The Federal Council dare not open this great subject of dispute. A plea of difference in religious faith is urged in several Cantons—in St. Gallen, in Graubünden, in Geneva, and in Aargau—where the population is more equally divided by the two confessions than in Fribourg; and the Council dares not brave a public conflict on such dangerous ground.

Each Canton and Half-canton is a separate

state, complete within itself, enjoying rights and offices derived from no exterior source, and holding various powers which she inherits from the past, and has not yet surrendered to the League. Not long ago each Canton had a separate coinage, and the raps and bats of one were not a legal tender in the next. Not long ago each Canton had an agent in Vienna, Rome, and Paris; and the greatest potentates sent ministers to Sarnen, Schwyz, and Zug. Each Canton claimed to treat with kings, and recognise all sovereign acts. For many years the Half-canton of Appenzell-inner-Rhoden would not recognise the French Revolution of 1830, and Louis Philippe was dethroned and dead before his agents in the Canton could obtain a hearing from their shepherd hosts.

Not long ago each Canton kept a custom-house on every road, and manned a tower at every bridge, at which to levy rates. Each load of grass and butt of wine, each sack of corn and pound of cheese, that passed her boundary was taxed. All fish that floated to her net was prize. Not long ago each Canton raised an army of her own, equipped and moved that army as she pleased, and lent her troops for hire to princes who could pay,—to Kings of France and Naples, and, still later, Popes of Rome. These several marks of sovereignty have been surrendered to the League. The cantonal mints, the cantonal embassies, the cantonal customs, and the cantonal armies—all these things are gone. Two remnants only of these sovereign powers remain : the right to levy certain rates on wine, called ohmgeld, at the frontiers of each Canton; and the right to keep on foot a half battalion of three hundred men.

Though stripped of these old marks of sovereignty, each Canton has a separate constitution, capital, and government. Each Canton has a parliament, a court of justice, and an executioner. Each Canton has the power of life and death. Each Canton makes and executes her laws.

Some Cantons fix the age at which a man begins to vote at twenty; others at eighteen; and one at least as low as sixteen. Where they have parliaments, the members of these parliaments are chosen by universal voting in the ballot-box. Each citizen is constrained to give his vote. A full majority of the votes recorded are required for an election. Every man is free to stand as candidate; every man is qualified to act as President; and every man is paid for service to a public cause.

Each Canton has a separate criminal code; and, even when the codes are pretty much the same in neighbouring Cantons, the procedure is unlike. Glarus and Unterwalden have no regular codes of criminal law; what passes in their courts for codes of law is old tradition, based on either clerical usages or ancient German rules. In Uri, Schwyz, and Unterwalden, certain crimes are punished by exposure in the pillory, by flogging, and by penance in the church. But these old forms of punishment are falling into disrepute. Geneva and the Jura districts have the penal codes of France. In Zürich, Aargau, Thurgau, and some other Cantons, modern codes have been adopted. Basel-stadt and Basel-land have different penal laws. The Appenzells have also different penal laws. But every Canton in the League displays some zeal in her amendment of the penal codes. In Zürich, Neufchâtel, and Fribourg, capital punishment has been abolished; and in other Cantons, which have not abolished capital punishment, the guillotine is substituted for the axe and sword. In Canton Bern the peasants cannot reconcile themselves to letting murderers escape with life; for in the Oberland, where roads are bad and hamlets spare, the highway-robber, they contend, is only to be daunted by the fear of death from adding murder to his other crimes.

CHAPTER XI.

CANTONAL RULE.

SOME Cantons rule themselves by means of parliaments, and some by means of popular votes; but every Canton rules herself.

About one half the Cantons and Half-cantons have no parliaments in the legal sense of words; and thinkers of much weight in democratic circles hold that government by means of deputies is on the wane—a stage of growth from which the world is passing into one of higher form.

At first, these thinkers say, you have Paternal Rule; then Royal or Imperial Rule; then Aristocratic or Parliamentary Rule. In what, they ask, does government by representatives, differ from government by counts and dukes? The voter has a right to choose his master, and obey that master's law. He has no right to rule himself. Beyond these methods lies a higher law—a final stage of growth—self-government in its noblest reach and simplest form—where every man is legislator, judge, and king.

Four groups are noted in these Swiss republics: first, a group which claims to be a Parliamentary Democracy; a second group which claims to be an Absolute Democracy; a third group which claims to be a Mixed Democracy; a fourth group which claims to be a Pure Democracy. In the first group stand Geneva, Vaud, Luzern, Fribourg, Aargau, Basel-stadt, Schaffhausen, Neufchâtel, Ticino. In the second group stand Uri, the two Appenzells, the two Unterwaldens, Glarus, Schwyz, and Zug. In the third group stand Graubünden, Bern, Thurgau, Valais, Basel-land, St. Gallen. Zürich stands alone in representing pure and perfect government, according to the newest democratic lights—where every man is legislator, judge, and king.

In each of the first group of Cantons—that of Parliamentary Democracy—a council, called the Grand Council, is elected by the voters having civil rights; that is to say, by males who have attained the legal age, and have not lost their rights by either emigration, idiocy, or crime. The voting is by ballot. This

Grand Council names a smaller body, called a State Council; and these two chambers choose, according to a form laid down, a President, who bears the title of Avoyer, Landammann, or Burgomeister, to conduct the government and execute the laws. A meeting of these members is the Cantonal Assembly. From their decisions there is no appeal. The three estates of President, State Council, and Grand Council, exercise the sovereign power.

Geneva is a fair example of this Parliamentary group. In 1847, a movement in the streets, which led to some hot fighting round the Hôtel de Ville, upset the old baronial constitution of Geneva, with its close, aristocratic guilds, and its restricted public suffrage. Every Genevese, male in sex, and twenty-one years old, acquired a right to vote for members of the Grand Council. When he has cast his vote into the urn, his functions cease. His Grand Council, consisting of one representative for every group of six hundred and sixty-six inhabitants, elects a State Council of seven persons, who may hold their offices ten years, and then are free to serve again. Some serve for life; but any of these members may be censured and removed by popular vote in the Grand Council. Such a vote is rare. A feudal tone prevails in the State Council, in which Antoine Carteret plays a leading part. Geneva has a rich and powerful burgher class, who claim a lofty ancestry, and talk of Conrad's barons as we English boast of William's knights. These burghers own the mansion of La Treille, the Terrace, and the Rue des Granges. Their wealth enables them to live without the cares of trade. They give themselves to art and books, and send into the world such specimens of their order as De Saussure, Neckar, De Candolle, and De la Rive. This class is rooted in the soil; and no amount of fighting in the streets can reach the rocks from which they grow; for learning, fame, and riches are original elements of public power. Geneva, therefore, is a Parliamentary Democracy, with a list of governing families, from which the citizen of twenty, with his rifle and his vote, enjoys the faculty of choosing who shall rule him at the Hôtel de Ville.

In the second group of Cantons—that of Absolute Democracy—the whole body of registered citizens meet in primary assemblies once a-year, to choose their magistrates, to quell disputes, to vote fresh taxes, to condemn offences and offenders, and to pass new laws. This primary assembly gathers on a summer Sunday—it is always on a Sunday—in some open place—a field, a market, or a grove. The voters come in arms. Each man is scrutinized by jealous eyes, and if his right to vote be challenged he must prove it on the spot. Such proof is easy to an honest man. What Commune is he from? Who are his witnesses? A Commune is a regiment, divided into companies and sections. Every man is counted in the rank and file. If any one is absent he is missed; and an intruder on the regiment will find in it no vacant place. The Cantonal Assembly is an army, not a mob. Unless a man be either pauper, bankrupt, criminal, or tramp, he has a right to vote. If he should prove to be a rogue—a fellow with no civic rights—it may go ill with him; the rogue is lucky to escape with life and limb. These primary assemblies of the Canton are extremely picturesque.

Take Uri as example of this second group. The men of Uri,—Catholic and Teutonic shepherds, carriers, guides, inn-keepers, foresters, with here and there a chamois-hunter,—give their franchise into no man's keeping. They remember Walter Fürst and William Tell. At every turn they see some record of the times when they were crushed like serfs and rose like men. What they have won by daring hand they mean to hold with sleepless eye. They give no council power to make and mend their laws, but lodge their sovereign right in the assembled Communes.

Not a rifle shot from Bürglen, in the Schächen Thal, where Tell was born, and where his chapel stands — beside a bridge across the Schächen, and between the road and river — lies a meadow, which for ages past has been a field of council for the men of Uri. Once a-year (first Sunday in the month of May, while yet the snow is often on the ground, and blocks of ice are rolling down the Reuss), the Landammann of Uri rides from Altdorf with a cavalcade; some cantonal troops with bands of music and the flag — a huge bull's head; some beadles clothed in black and yellow; and two ancient Switzers carrying on their poles two buffalo-horns, the antique cognizance of Uri. From the upper Reuss pour down the men of Andermatt and Wasen; through the Maderaner Thal come out the men of Bristen and Stössi; by the Schächen Thal march in the men of Bürglen and Spiringen; across the Reuss arrive the men of Seedorf and Attinghausen. Every man in Uri, twenty years of age, and wearing neither monkish hood nor priestly frock, is bound to show himself this day. A stage is thrown up in the council field; the buffalo-horns are raised; a bugle sounds the assembly; and the Landammann takes his seat. This session of a single day begins. An usher reads the list of matters to be done. Some regiment is to be raised in strength; a road is to be made, a torrent dyked, a forest thinned; some tax is to be laid; an officer is to be punished; perhaps some law is to be changed. Each orator is called upon to speak. His plan is heard and judged. The vote is open, given by show of hands. One scheme finds favour and another not. The losing cause has no appeal. When every vote is taken, and the business of the day is done, these kings of Uri slake their thirst with beer, pull down their stage, and wend their several ways towards home with patriotic pipe and song.

Graubünden is a fair sample of the third group; that of Mixed Democracy. This Canton is a mixture of original sort; for out of ancient Greece and modern Caucasus, no rival can be set against it for varieties of race and creed, of law and speech. The country has no name, nor is her nickname of the Grisons known at Chur. She calls herself Grau-bünden—League of Grey Coats; Gottes-haus bünden—League of Holy Church; Zehn Gerichtes-bünden—League of Ten Courts. But half her people never use these names. These people are of Celtic race and speak a southern tongue. To them the leagues are Lia Grischa, Lia de Ca Dè, and Lia dellas desch Dretturas. In and out among the pine-woods and cascades, these northern men and southern men are mingled; here a Celtic village and a Roman porch, there a Teutonic hamlet and a Gothic spire. The Celts are mainly Catholic, the Teutons mainly Protestant; but creeds are not defined by boundaries of race and speech. Dissentis is Catholic; Ilanz is Protestant; Chur is mixed. The Lutherans of Chur are traders living in the lower town; the Romanists are rich proprietors, who dwell within the precincts of the Bishop's court. In all, this Canton has some forty thousand Catholics to fifty thousand Protestants; but they are too much mixed in towns and villages to live apart, like Basel-stadt and Basel-land.

In dropping from the Ober Alp to Chur, you pass a line of feudal and ecclesiastical remains; old castles on the heights, old abbeys in the flats; and everywhere you find some trace of ancient counts and knights. At Dissentis, you have the Benedictine abbey—now a school for boys; at Chur, you find the Convent of St. Lucius, now a cantonal school; at Dieni, Castelberg, and Trins, you see the ruins of old fortresses; at Laax and Chur, you note old houses, carved with coat and shield.

For ages this wild region was the prey of counts and knights, who trampled on the serfs, and men who were not serfs, until the villagers sprang up, and formed a rustic league in every district for defence. These district-leagues extended into circles, and while every hamlet chose to rule itself, with only scant regard to what occurred elsewhere, the pressure of events compelled the rustics to extend their bands. Three greater leagues were formed in time: (1) the Grey League (Grau-bünden—from the peasant's homespun), with its seat in Trons; (2) the Church League (Gottes-haus bund), with its seat in Chur;

and (3) the Ten Courts' League (Zehn Gerichtesbünden), with its seat in Mayenfeld. In name, these rustic leagues have past away; but they remain in spirit and in fact. The Canton is divided into fourteen districts, thirty-nine circles, two hundred and five communes. Each circle is a separate republic. Chur is called the capital; and here the deputies of the circles meet. The Council sits in secret, and conducts the public business with unsparing hand. But then these deputies have to march in harmony with the general will. They must not lay a tax, they must not change a law, without the popular assent. All matters of importance are remitted to the districts, and a public vote of peasants may upset the wisest plans conceived in Chur.

Of Pure Democracy the one example yet is Zürich; and the case of Canton Zürich must be treated as a thing apart.

CHAPTER XII.

CANTON ZÜRICH.

A BRIGHT old city on a fresh green lake—white houses nestling in the midst of trees; quaint streets, arcades, and spires; grim minsters looking down on shop and stall; wide quays and bridges, piers and water-mills; old convents, walls, and towers; new colleges, hotels, and railway-lines; the records of a thousand years, the fancies of a passing day; a church of Charles the Great, a palace of the modern arts; one river leading from the lake; a second river rushing from the hills; around you mounds and crests, here rolling outward to the Adlis-berg, there straining upward to the Albis chain; each hill with vineyards at her base and village belfry on her top; and in the front, beyond the stretch of shining lake, a rugged line of alps, all swathed and lit with snow—is Zürich city, capital of

Zürich Canton, and a paradise of learning and of learned men.

Some natives speak of Zürich as the Swiss Athens; men who live in books and have their hearts inflamed with ancient Greeks. For Zürich is the centre of a Switzer's intellectual life. Among her literary and artistic circles, she can boast academies of art and music; institutes of science and of law; botanic gardens, public libraries and museums; a society of public usefulness; a Grütli club, an Alpine club, a reading club, a natural-history club; societies of commerce and of agriculture; many hospitals, retreats, asylums; a society of antiquities; a public garden on the lake; a theatre; a temple of freemasons; many Church unions; and a hundred colleges and schools. The University is here; the Polytechnic is here; the anatomical school is here; the cantonal schools and burgher schools are here. Yon shining edifice on the slope, above the Heretics Tower, is a palace of the practical arts. This block abutting on the minster is the ladies' school. Those buildings in the tulip-trees are secondary schools. In the Virgin's quarter, near the Town Hall, stand the city schools for boys. On every side, in almost every street, you find a school; a primary school, a secondary school, a supplementary school; day schools, evening schools; schools for the blind; schools for the deaf and dumb (all models of their kind); industrial schools, commercial schools, linguistic schools: yes, schools of every sort and size, excepting actual pauper schools. For Canton Zürich has no paupers born and bred; no paupers known and labelled as a class apart. Some poor she has; but they are few in number; not, as with ourselves, a state within the State.

A prosperous country stretches round the city and reflects her life; a Canton small in size compared with Bern, Graubünden, Vaud, and Valais; but teeming with a brave, enduring race; a people full of labour, song, and fight; a little rough in speech and hard in style, as men who know their worth are apt to be; yet patient in their strength, disposed to work with nature, not against her laws. The land is lovely in itself, and made more lovely still by art. Fair lakes are brightened by the works of man; by latteen sail and puff of silver cloud, no less than by the cheery range of garden, châlet, wood, and spire. Low hills are tamed to vineyards, while the higher grounds are fat with fruit. Above these knolls, on which the grapes and medlars seem to ripen against nature, start the bergs and spits all green with wood; and straining up their sides, and flowing from their feet, broad belts of pasture land, on which vast herds of cattle range to browse. So far as art can reach, these mountain slopes are cleared and fenced for use. A craft, a will, a strength, but seldom seen in man's affairs, are noted in this Canton; not in one part only, and in one thing only, but in every part and every thing alike. The climate is not good. The average warmth is lower than in Kent. Sharp winds sweep down the gullies and across the lake. Yon peaks are noted for their wintry storms, and one great breadth of alp in front of Zürich bears the name of Windgelle—screaming wind. The soil is poor and gritty; three parts pounded rock to one part vegetable mould. Yet when the best is made of it, how much that best can do! Observe the peasant's shed, the pastor's porch, the farmer's field: how clean that shed, how bright that porch, how orderly that field! You see no heaps of mess, you smell no hidden filth. Each article is in its place; and order reigns by virtue of some natural law. These roads are wide, these bridges strong, these waters fenced. The snows melt rapidly in Canton Zürich; yet the floods, being guided and contained by dykes, roll down their beds, and through their overflows, without much hurt; while in some neighbouring and neglected Cantons they are dashing mills to pieces, drowning goats and sheep, and tearing forests from the ground. In small things and in great you find these proofs of active thought and ready hand. Just peep into this bit of ground; a common garden, with the usual herbs and roots, the usual flowers and seeds. Each bed, each tree, each plant, is treated by itself, as though it were a child. Observe how every branch is pruned, how every leek is watered, and how every gourd is trained. You need not marvel at the cherries on that tree. Here in the corner climbs a vine. The summer heat is on her leaves, and what a promise of the blood-red grapes to come!

The country all round Zürich is a garden, watered by innumerable springs and lakes. These springs and lakes are trained, with Oriental craft, to flow about the orchards and potato-fields. Though mostly built of stone, the farms are painted of a cheery yellow, pink, and white. These walks are planted, and these roads well kept. Each

I

house appears to stand in its own grounds. No poor are to be seen about the roads, save here and there some Swabian tramp, some Savoy beggar, or some pilgrim to St. Meinrad's cell. No Züricher is homeless; hardly any Züricher is poor. In driving on these roads, you hear at every turn the song of life and work—the woodman felling trees, the milkmaid bringing home her pail, the cobbler stitching at his stall, the miller grinding at his wheel—all chirping at their task the live-long day. The secret of this gracious look of things in Canton Zürich is, that every man enjoys an independent place.

These labourers have an interest in the soil they till. No ballast for a man like that of having a little earth—his own—about his feet. These rustics own the cottages in which they live—the ground on which they toil. Though peasants born and bred, they understand their rights. They have been long at school, and know the history of their canton and their country. Every man among them has been taught his civic duties —has been schooled and drilled into a man. A child, he conned his lessons in the Virgin's quarter of the town; a youth, he marched and wheeled on the parade; a man, he casts his vote in the electoral urn, and scores his bull's eye at the Wollis Hofen butts.

Each peasant owns, besides his house and field, a rifle and a vote.

No sleepy hollow, where a shepherd feeds his flock, a craftsman plies his trade, without one thought beyond the summer heat and winter cold, is Canton Zürich; but a fierce and busy agora, in which all news are searched, all questions put, all answers canvassed in their length and depth. The heat of life is felt in every vein. All forces here seem vital forces; pulse and brain beat time together; and the hearts of men dilate with the abounding tides. Democracy is not a name—a form of words—a label on a book of laws; it is a fact. Each unit in the body politic is a living force. At dawn, a man gets up to work; while sitting at his loom he thinks; some grievance in the code arrests him; he imparts his fancy to a neighbour; in a week a new discussion may arise. A thousand projects agitate men's minds, and keep them in a state of civic health; from Federal questions down to Communal questions, and from problems of the church and state to trifles of the streets and stalls. But most of all, men talk and fight about political forms.

In one sense, Canton Zürich is conservative. She clings with limpet-like tenacity to her main ideas—her republican faith, her Federal duty, her religious life; but in a lower plane she is of revolutionary cities the most revolutionary. Every twenty years, or so, she sets about revising her fundamental pact. Men yet living can remember five or six fundamental laws in Zürich, from the semi-feudal constitution overthrown in 1831, to the new and perfect system of democracy set up in 1869.

Some forty years ago, some Feudal families in Zürich, boasting of descent from ancient vogts and bailiffs, held the whip; an aristocracy of wealth and learning, fenced about with privilege and immunity, and holding by the right of birth all avenues to political power. By a set of public movements, and with scarcely any bloodshed in her streets, these Feudal families were displaced. It is the genius of the Züricher to gain his ends by short and easy steps. A man of order, he contents himself with action in the polling-booths. One day he gains a point; another day he gains a point. In time his revolution has been made, and public order has not been disturbed.

The University was in the lower town, in old monastic lodgings, dreary, small, and dark. The Liberals wished to plant it out on open ground, in sunshine, on the crest, where every eye could catch a glimpse of it. The Feudalists would have no change; the Liberals beat them, and the University was removed.

Old walls and towers surrounded, cramped, and closed the town. The Liberals wished to pull them down, to let in air and light, to build a railway station near the city gates, to fill the ditch, and turn the glacis into terraces and schools. The Feudalists opposed this change; the Liberals beat them, and the walls came down, excepting only two or three old towers retained as picturesque memorials of the past.

The constitution was too feudal in its character to please a democratic people holding guns and votes. A public meeting was convened in 1867 to ask for a revision. What the Liberals wanted was a more direct relation of the voters to the government; a right to choose the State Council as well as the Grand Council; a veto on financial projects; and a larger influence over church and school. The Feudalists protested; but the Liberals beat them on appeal, and then the Cantonal constitution was revised.

CHAPTER XIII.

PURE DEMOCRACY.

IN the Pure Democracy set up by her new constitution, Zürich left behind her old principle of Parliamentary Rule, and ceased, so far as Cantonal objects are concerned, to be a representative state. Her government is now direct. The people name their officers; the people choose their judges; and the people make their laws. The deputies are clerks, not kings. Each voter has a share, direct and visible, in public acts. He hires a servant, in his deputy, to report on such and such a case, and draft a bill in such and such a sense. But he invests this servant with no plenary powers. In all affairs of consequence he gives his vote with his own hand and tongue. He only is the sovereign prince, and in his sphere he only reigns and rules.

In front of the new constitution of Canton Zürich stand these words:—'The People of

Canton Zürich, in the exercise of their sovereign rights, give themselves the following constitution.'

Sixty-five articles succeed in groups.

The first group—articles 1 to 18—deal with Political Principles.

1. The public power resides in the whole body of citizens, not in any part of it. This public power is used directly by all citizens having civic rights; and indirectly by such citizens as may be either chosen officers of state, or hired as servants of the State.

2. All citizens are equal, in a legal and political sense, unless deprived by law of civil and political rights. Article 18 defines the causes for suspending civil and political rights, as lunacy, degrading crime, fraudulent bankruptcy, and receipt of public alms.

3. Speech is free; printing is free. The right of meeting and associating is guaranteed. No limit can be put upon this freedom of speaking, printing, meeting, and associating, other than such as springs from the rights enjoyed by all. A true statement, published with an honest motive, is not to be regarded as a libel by the courts of law.

4. The State defends all honest private

rights. The State may seize in case of public need; but compensation must be given; the details settled in the proper courts.

5. The punishment of death is abolished. Chains and manacles are forbidden in the public jails. The criminal laws are to be softened.

7. A man's personal liberty is secured. No man may be arrested save on proper warrants, as prescribed by special laws. Imprisonment for debt is abolished. No means of forcing a confession are allowed. The state must satisfy in money any injury done to a citizen by false arrest.

8. A man's house is his castle, only to be entered either by his own consent or by a legal writ. This legal writ must specify the object of the visitation, and the extent to which it may be carried. In case of public danger these restrictions are not binding; but the officers must answer for their acts.

10. Every public functionary is responsible to the Canton and the city, as well as to private persons, in accordance with the law.

11. No office can be held for life. Authorities must be renewed in block and not in parts. Father and son, two brothers, father-in-law and son-in-law, two brothers-in-law, may not serve

together on any administrative board, nor on any judicial bench. A member of the Council is chosen for three years. An officer is chosen, and a functionary is appointed, for three years. A judge is named for six years; and a notary for the same.

13. Election of officers is by ballot, whether the election is in Canton or in city. Municipalities may also use this form of voting.

14. Settlement is free. Any Switzer, on performing certain legal acts, may fix himself in any place, and get the local rights of citizenship. A Commune can only charge a moderate entering fee. No higher taxes can be levied on a stranger than on natives. A refusal to admit a claimant must be justified by evidence that his ways of life are dangerous to public morals. If a settler is expelled, this act of rigour must be justified by evidence that his presence is a danger to the State.

15. Civil marriage and clerical marriage are placed on the same legal ground. No fees are to be paid to either pastor, priest, or mayor.

16. A man enters on the enjoyment of his civic right with the close of his twentieth year. These civil rights include the faculty of contracting

debts, of voting at elections, and of serving in any public office.

A second group—Articles 19 to 27—deal with Economical Principles.

19. Every one must pay his rates. Communal and burgher property is taxed. An income-tax and property-tax are laid on an ascending scale. Small fortunes are exempt. The tax on property may be doubled on the greater income. Lands and goods inherited are taxed on a progressive scale, according to the distance of relationship and to the sum bequeathed. Large fortunes are abominable in a pure democracy. No corporate body is exempt. The tax on salt is to be lowered. No fresh tax of any kind is to be put on common articles of food.

21. All crafts are open, saving in so far as they are limited by law. Any one can practise a profession. Art, science, industry, and trade are free to all.

22. The Communes have charge of the poor; the State assists in case of need.

23. The State approves and aids co-operative societies, resting on the principle of self-help. Laws are made for the protection of working men.

25. The State assists the Communes to repair the roads.

26. The State controls all railway lines.

27. The State provides an outfit for the men who join the Cantonal flag.

A third group—articles 28 to 36—deals with Popular Rights.

28. The people, with the help of the Cantonal Council, chosen by themselves, assume the legislative power.

The people vote on every bill proposed to them, and either make it law or cast it off. From this decision there is no appeal. The people have a right to offer measures for debate. The people may demand—first, the passing of a new law; second, the amendment of an old law; third, the full and absolute cancel of a law. These rights are to be used according to the legal forms.

A single person may propose a bill, and send it to the Cantonal Council; if a third part of that Council should support his view, the subject must be laid before the people for decision. When a private person sends a question to the Cantonal Council for debate, he has a right to come before that Council to explain his views, if twenty-five members think he should be heard.

Five thousand voters may insist on putting any question to a popular vote. A number of Communal meetings, representing five thousand voters, may insist. The Cantonal Council must return their question on the paper. No delay will be allowed. In every case the Cantonal Council have the right to offer an opinion on the bill proposed, and, if they choose, may place before the people a counter-project of their own.

30. A popular vote takes place in every spring and autumn. Every act must be submitted to the popular will. No act is legal till it has been sanctioned by this public poll. In urgent cases, the Cantonal Council may propose to take an extra vote. The Council may submit a bill in one of two forms, either as a whole, or part by part. The voting is by ballot in each Commune; every citizen is bound to cast his card into the box. A man must answer, Yea or Nay. All matters to be voted on must be printed and dispersed a month before the poll is held. An absolute majority of voices makes or mars.

31. The Cantonal Council shape the public

bills, command the public force (except so far as it is under Federal obligation), execute the laws, elect their officers, and exercise the right of mercy.

32. A Councillor, as public officer, receives a daily stipend, with a sum of money for expenses.

36. The two members of the State Council who are sent to Bern must be elected by the people, forming for this Federal act a single district. The members of the National Council who are also sent to Bern must be elected (as they were under the old constitution) by the people, forming for this purpose a single district. These two elections must be held at the same time. The service of these Federal delegates is for three years.

A fourth group—articles 37 to 55—deals with the Administration.

37. The Executive Power consists of seven members, called a Council of Government. These governors are elected by the people, forming one electoral district, at the same time with the Cantonal Council.

38. These seven governors appoint a President and a Vice-president for a year.

39. No man having an appointment with a fixed salary can be a governor.

41. The governors appoint a public prosecutor.

A fifth group—articles 56 to 61—deals with Crime and Justice.

56. A judgment of the law-courts cannot be set aside. The Cantonal Council have the power of mercy; but the administration cannot modify the verdict given. Political crimes, including press offences, must be tried by jury. Courts of arbitration are allowed.

A public officer is charged with process in a case of debt.

A sixth group—articles 62 to 64—deals with Public Education and Ecclesiastical Affairs.

62. The general education of the people, and the republican education of the citizens, is the business of the State. In order to increase the professional and productive power of all classes, the Cantonal schools are to be extended and improved. The training must be better, and the period of instruction longer. The Universities and colleges are to be brought into more perfect harmony with modern life. Their scientific character must be retained; and

they must be connected in their courses with the Cantonal schools.

Primary instruction is obligatory and gratuitous. The State, together with the Communes, will supply the funds. The Communes have the management of primary schools, assisted by a district School Board.

63. Liberty of faith, of worship, and of teaching, is established. Civil rights and civil duties have no dependence on religious creeds. No force (as excommunication) can be used against communities or individuals. The National Church (that is to say, the Evangelical Church), and other religious corporations, rule themselves within the law and under the supreme control of the State.

64. The Church Communes elect their own pastors, and the School Communes their own teachers. The State endows the pastors, and she pays a portion of the teacher's salary. These pastors and these teachers are elected to their functions for a term of six years; at the end of which they may be re-elected if the people choose. This rule applies to the Romanist Communes, not less than to the Evangelical Communes.

The seventh group—article 65—deals with the subject of any future revision of the constitution. It is provided that the people may at any time, according to the legal mode, revise this fundamental pact, either in the mass or in any of the parts.

CHAPTER XIV.

A REVOLUTION.

In the struggles of the Radical party with the Feudal party, following the adoption of this pact, Johannes Sieber, until then a man unknown, came quickly to the front, took up the popular flag, and made himself at once a type of the new era, and an incarnation of the radical cause.

Johannes Sieber was the master of a village-school at Uster, on the Greifen lake, some dozen miles from Zürich. Uster was a feudal hamlet, now it is a weaving station. On the knoll above the weavers' houses rise the remnants of a castle, which are turned to use as court-house, jail, and inn. A tower, on which the weavers drink their beer, commands the lake below, and in the distance sweeps the peaks and crests of Schwyz. Near by a group of factories frets the sky, and smoking chimneys overtop both feudal tower and Gothic spire. In Uster,

Sieber was employed in teaching rustics how to read and sing. Like nearly all his class he was a politician of advancing views. His school was in the shadow of that ancient pile; a living proof that victory is with the popular cause. He was no learned pundit; he had taken no degree; but he was full of speech and pluck; and, more than all, he had the sense to see that this great struggle of the popular and conservative parties turned upon the public schools.

'You see the fruit, but not the root,' my host explains to me, as we are driving past the Cantonal schools; 'these youngsters streaming from the steps are like the vines on yonder wall; they flourish in our soil, but draw their being from a distant source. We Switzers are not poets and inventors; we are homely folk; but then we know a good thing when we see it, and are quick to try if it will suit us. I am not an old man yet; but in my youth you might have passed from Basel to Ticino and not have seen a decent public school.'

'You have not let the grass grow where you tread.'

'Not only is our scheme of State instruction new, it is Germanic, and not Latin, in its origin, its spirit, and its plan. We date our university in Zürich from an early time; but in that early time the church was always in a teacher's mind. A teacher seldom thought of civil life. He was a priest; he wished to make his pupils priests. His school was part of some religious house; some priory, some abbey, where the ruler was in holy orders. His instruction was devoted to a single purpose. Priests required some letters, and they got some. Girls required no letters, and they got none. Females had no chance of learning how to read and write, except through private means and at enormous cost. A man who wished his girls to learn was forced to hire a priest and lodge him in his house.'

'The change came on, you think, with the revolt from Rome?'

'With Martin Luther. Rome was pagan in her spirit. She would never give her system of instruction to all classes. Luther was our source of civic life. He was the first to claim that public teaching should extend to all; to rich and poor, to male and female, and to bond and free. Yes, Luther is the father of democracy. He, more than any Switzer, shaped our politics and framed our laws.'

In England, Luther's efforts in the cause of education are not known so well as his attacks on Rome. He meant to build a new world on the ruins he was making; and the world he wished to raise was one of right and reason, not of simple trust. He wanted men to read and think, assured that men who read and think will never drop into a stagnant faith. All men, he therefore said, must learn to read. It is the business of society to see that none fall off and lose their souls for lack of light. He taught the two great doctrines of the democratic party—that female education is of equal moment to the State with male, and that the State should force all citizens to attain a certain grade in either public schools or private schools.

'The fruit is here, the root is yonder,' says my host. 'We know the truth; our system is Germanic; and we feed it daily from the parent source. Although we are a nation of schoolmasters—Pestalozzi was born in Zürich—yet our leading lights are German. Pestalozzi, Fellenberg, and other Switzers have been great in detail, not in principle. Our great reformers come from the original source. We start with Luther, and we end with Scherr.'

Scherr—who is Scherr, some reader asks, that he should stand in line with Luther? Scherr is not a man of name, and yet his work was good and he performed it well. In Zürich he is dearly loved. As Luther gave to public teaching a popular spirit, Scherr endowed it with a popular form. Scherr is the actual founder of the system now prevailing in Canton Zürich; and in no slight measure is the author of her wealth, intelligence, and fame. She loves him all the more that she was cruel to him while he lived, and torn with anguish for him when he died.

Born in the small village of Hohenrechberg, in the kingdom of Würtemberg, Thomas Scherr received his training in the public school, and feeling a vocation for the teacher's office, studied pedagogy as an art, and got appointed to a desk. His fame soon spread abroad; for he was not a teacher only, but a special teacher, with ideas of his own. Promoted to the mastership of a deaf-and-dumb institution, he arrested wide attention by his plan for teaching mutes to speak. At twenty-four he came to Zürich, where the state of education was below the mark. Here he got appointed to the Blind School, which he thoroughly reformed, and with such full approval of the city that the Government increased his school by adding to it a department for the deaf and dumb, in order that his theories of teaching might be fully tried. Before that day—the time was 1825 to 1836—all teachers of the deaf and dumb had been content with the opinion of De l'Epée and the Abbé Sicard, that the only way to teach a mute is by the *hand*. Watson in England, Heinicke in Germany, Clerc in the United States, were followers of that method. Scherr had other thoughts. No man, he found, is naturally mute. A child is dumb because he is first deaf, and does not hear articulate sounds. But may he not be taught articulation through the eye? Scherr thought he might. He dropped the finger-alphabet, and tried to teach his pupils to articulate in letters, syllables, and words. Articulate sounds are formed by breathing through the lips and teeth, along the palate and the tongue, and all the movements of these organs, while the sounds are issuing, may be *seen*. A little care and patience, and the pupil imitates these movements, and acquires the gift of speech. A double end is gained; for while he learns the art of breathing words, he also learns the art of reading them. A class of mutes who can distinguish what the master says can also trace the accents on each other's lips—by sight. The power of interchanging thought, if not so rapid as in men with all their senses, is complete. A great success attended Scherr. Some pupils learned to speak with ease, and many learned to speak a bit. In six years he had made his ground so sure that, when the Canton wished to frame a better code, he was elected to the Education Council, and intrusted by that Council with the task of drawing up a general law.

Public codes are common now, for every Canton in the League has framed a public code; but in the days of Scherr such things were new and strange, and the Feudal party, urged by Dr. Bluntschli (one of the aristocrats whose ancestors had governed Zürich long before she joined the Forest Cantons), led the innovator an uneasy life.

Scherr wished this business of education to be made a business of the State. He held that every one should go to school, that every village should provide a school, that every citizen should take his share in managing a school, and that the parents should be pressed to visit and inspect the school. He wished to see the school a home, and hoped to call the family spirit to his help. To him no subject was so serious as the school. He meant the world to see things as he saw them; and he hoped by means of public festivals to bring the highest interests of the Canton on the public schools.

One part of his reform the Canton put in force without delay. The want of Zürich was the want of Europe—teachers who were fit to teach. Except in Germany, no such artists in tuition could be found; and Scherr proposed to found a training college near the city, where selected youths, of either sex, might be instructed in this difficult and important art.

Four miles from Zürich city, on a slip of vineyard mirrored in the waters, stands the pretty thorpe of Küsnacht. In this pretty thorpe his training college was erected. Three years later Küsnacht was a place of name and fame, and men from every part of Europe flocked to see the master at his work. An impetus was given to teaching in all countries; more than all in the Teutonic Cantons of the League. As teacher, Scherr was very great. His lessons on the forms of speech, and on the graces of expression, were remarkable for neatness, brilliancy, and point.

With boys and girls he had a vast success; his manner was convincing, and his power of illustration and comparison was endless. Scherr was happy in his work, and all, except the Feudal party, who were open enemies of public education, were extremely proud of Scherr.

The wider grew his fame, the sharper grew his pain. A cry rose up against him that he wished to ruin trade by driving every boy and girl to school. A hundred manufacturers declared that they would have to close their shops. They could not carry on their works. Their industry would perish, and their capital be lost. If Scherr were suffered to go on they must remove their mills to Cantons where such fools were not allowed to tamper with the laws of trade. They might be driven away to France.

Scherr answered that the city was extending on all sides; five hundred new houses were being built; the streets were cleaner, quieter than of yore; the port was filled with an increasing fleet of boats; and thousands of foreign artisans were coming to the town for work. New public buildings were commenced; the ancient walls were overthrown; new terraces and gardens rose on either side the lake. New book-shops opened.

Singing-clubs were formed. A theatre was built. Some fine hotels were added to the town. The Dom was put into repair. A higher spiritual plane was reached.

The Feudal party were convicted, not convinced; and when the next reflux of passion brought them into power, they wreaked their hatred on the man, although they were not strong enough to stay his work. Scherr died in exile from the Canton he had made his own.

Johannes Sieber seized the golden chance. A master of a school like Scherr, he found the liberal sentiment was with his class. The name and cause of Scherr were dear to all; and Sieber wrote that name, that cause, upon his flag. The Liberals took him for their leader, and the fight being won, they carried him from his desk at Uster into Government House in Zürich, where he holds, under the Pure Democracy, the two chief offices of this Canton—President of the Council, and Director of the Education Board.

CHAPTER XV.

POPULAR VICTORIES.

SOME articles in the newest Zürich code arrest the eye at once, as being the latest phase of democratic hope and faith. Two points have been established in this fundamental pact:—(1) the Relation of the People to the State, and (2) the Relation of the People to the Church.

The people have assumed all powers. Great Councils and State Councils are no longer what they were, and party government is swept away. No parliaments meet to choose the rulers and to make the laws. Canton Zürich is herself a parliament. These Zürich people choose their governors as American people choose their presidents—by one direct and universal vote. Seven governors are elected at a single poll. A governor can only stay three years in office; he must then retire; and it is not supposed that he will stand again. The spirit of the pact is change.

In the sphere of legislation this reserve of powers is more complete than in the sphere of government. No act is valid till the people have pronounced their verdict. In theory this reference to the people (Referendum) is a kind of veto, like the vetos exercised in monarchies by kings and queens; in practice it is something more than kings and queens can claim. The right is absolute and imperious. A right of veto is no more than that of raising an objection, more or less, of days or months. It gives no power to modify a bill; it gives no power to substitute a bill. It is a pure negation. But a Zürich voter is an autocrat. He has a right, not only to reject, but to propose. He may suggest a bill; and, by assent of certain of his fellows, can insist on having his proposal laid before the Canton. Every Züricher enjoying civil rights is a member of the national parliament, by which his rulers are elected and his laws are made. A Züricher is commoner, peer, and king in one.

More curious than this reference to the people in affairs of state, is the position taken up by pure democracy towards the church.

In England, France, and Italy, the radicals are mostly — though not all — in favour of a thorough separation of the church and state; but such is not a Züricher's idea; for in this republic men perceive, not only that religion is a part of public life, but that the church is an integral portion of the state. To drive the church away from the state is not to overthrow the church. These Switzers understand that a state church is a Lay church. To cast away the church as something alien to the state and civil life, is to abandon all control of the most vital force and passion in the human heart.

These radicals hold on, therefore, to the doctrine of a National Church. Being Evangelical in opinion, they declare the Evangelical Church to be the National Church. All forms of worship are allowed; all forms of worship recognized by the Canton are endowed; all congregations regulate their own affairs, within the law and under state control. Each Commune chooses her own priest and pastor for a term of years.

A church so ruled presents to them the very model of a national and democratic church.

When Sieber, carried into office on the crests of this pacific revolution, came to live at Government House, he found himself opposed by two strong parties in the city; first, the Feudalists, whom he had beaten at the poll, and the Professors, whom his victory seemed to threaten in their chairs.

In Radical creeds no article is held with firmer faith than that which says, no public office should be held for life. In every Canton of Switzerland this article is urged against appointments in the pulpits and the schools, no less than in the principal offices of state. If you would have the best men in the best places, say the Radicals, you must change them often. Sieber, as a Radical leader, sent to Government House in order to complete the changes introduced into the Cantonal code, proposed a bill to amend the laws appointing teachers and professors to their posts.

The old laws gave such posts for life, without regard to changes in the men, the methods, and the means. No reason, say the Radicals, can be given for such a rule, which came into existence through the church and not the state. The doctrine, once a priest always a priest, implied, once

a teacher always a teacher, while the teacher and
the priest were one. But now that rule is changed;
a priest is not a teacher, and a teacher not a priest.
A layman has no sacred privilege to plead. He is
a man, as every citizen is a man; and what was
suffered in the cleric, who received his mandate
from a spiritual power, need not be suffered in
the laic, who derives his mandate from a temporal power. All liberal Zürichers desire a
change, not only for the public good, but for
the good of teachers and professors. But the
teachers and professors are of different minds
respecting Sieber's plan. The teachers are in
favour of a change, and Sieber is no other than
their mouthpiece on the Board. No art, they
urge, stands still, and that of teaching is a swiftly
growing art. From Fellenberg to Scherr the distance is immense. A man who holds his post for
life has no inducement to excel; good teachers
have no chance against bad teachers; and improvements in the method have to wait for years.
They, therefore, pray the Council to declare by
law that every desk and chair in Zürich shall be
held for some fixed term of years—say two years,
four years, six years—and shall then be filled
again by public choice. Who can question the

sincerity of persons pleading for reform against their seeming interests? All these teachers held their posts for life. Their prayer is granted, and the teachers will in future hold their desks six years. At every term a fresh election must take place; and every teacher in the Canton hails this verdict as a victory for his class.

The great professors take another line. These learned persons live on higher planes, and have no personal objects to attain by public strife. Engaged in work which will not perish with the hour, they turn with some disdain from what is passing in the streets, to ask of what is new in Bunsen's crucible and what is written in the latest book by Mill. They live in their own world—a high, serene, and prosperous world for them—well fed, well housed, and easy in their minds. Not so the teachers of a lower grade. A teacher, with a cottage, garden-plot, and thirty pounds a-year; his home an alpine valley, with no outlet to the world; his fortune, like his home, without a second hope; is likely to be swayed by popular passions, to indulge in dreams, to fancy he has wrongs, to enter into contests which excite his blood, and, if successful, bring

L

him to the front. A great professor cannot rise. He is a duke; he walks in purple; nay, he wears the crown. To be elected on the Council would be loss of rank. What a republic can do for such men as Kinkel, Vögelin, Gusserow, Behn-Eschenburg, and others, has been done. A teacher, like Johannes Sieber, fagging in his village school at Uster, finds that public life has many charms and chances. What has such a man to lose? What he may gain is proved. A village teacher may become a Governor, may preside at Council meetings, and may live at Government House.

Such rising of the lower ranks against the higher is regarded by the University men with an unfriendly eye. 'Good sort of man, this Sieber,' they remark, 'if he would only keep his place; but a Director of the Board of Education—why, the fellow has not taken his degree!' When Sieber comes to live at Government House, the great professors whisper to each other, 'Why, this fellow wants to be our master, and he has not taken his degree!' The fact is certain, and the learned men wax high in wrath.

Much trouble grows between the city and the University. For several years a course of winter lectures has been given by great professors in the city hall; a course on special subjects, treated in a popular style. These lectures have been well received; the public pay six francs a seat to hear them; the city lend the hall; the lecturer gives his service; and the money taken at the doors is paid in lump to the authorities of the University and Polytechnic for the adornment of their common pile. Much painting on the walls, and many figures in the niches, are required to clothe the public rooms with beauty; and the funds which come from lecturing keep an artist at this work. Last winter this delightful course was stopped, to the regret of every class alike—professor, citizen, and stranger in the town. When men like Kinkel lecture on the arts, when men like Keller lecture on the water-folk, the world is glad to hear them, and the course is sure to pay. Why are they stopped? 'It is the war in France,' says one; 'It is the small-pox,' says another. There is something in the air; the moon comes nearer to the earth; the spheres are out of tune; the pulse of party life is strong; men cannot act together; and the city and the University retire into their several camps. But time has laid this strife; and in these present winter months the learned men have stooped once more from their Olympian heights.

The fact is, they are beating Sieber and the democrats. Unlike the teachers, these professors will not yield on what the new and pure republic holds to be a cardinal doctrine—that of short appointments to all public seats. Some hate this principle of Reference to the People; but the matter does not touch them closely, and they yield to it with some reserve. Subjecting chairs of Greek and Hebrew, chemistry and mathematics, to a popular vote, renewed from time to time, appears to them absurd. This democratic principle is applied at the Polytechnic, where the chairs are only held six years. The great professors fear it may invade the University, and empty half the higher seats. They will not yield to Sieber's project, and the Radical party, rather than disturb a University which is their noblest pride, consent to strike this article out of Sieber's bill.

Amended so far, Sieber's bill is law. Professors in the University are the only officers of the new republic, who retain their posts for life. On every other class—on Pastor, President, Captain, Councillor—the new and pure republic exercises sovereign power. Each officer must yield his place, and take his chances of a second choice. Was it not said just now that a professor in the University of Zürich is a duke?

CHAPTER XVI.

THE LEAGUE.

THE Swiss League consists of twenty-five republics; nineteen Cantons, six Half-cantons; which agree for certain purposes, mainly of defence, to form a single commonwealth, with one assembly, one executive power.

This League of Cantons is a growth of time. Before the thirty-three famous patriots met in Grütli to exchange their pledges, acts of union had been signed by some of the Cantons, and the very words of Grütli, 'All for each, and each for all,' had been exchanged by them on oath. Luzern had signed an act of mutual help with Bern, and those who signed that act were called Companions of the Oath. In 1291, Canton Schwyz and Canton Uri formed a league with the Half-canton of Unterwalden-nidwald, to which the second Half-canton, Unterwalden-obwald, afterwards adhered. They took the vow of 'All for each and each for all.' Sixty days after the swearing of this oath of friendship, Canton Zürich entered into union for defensive purposes with Canton Schwyz and Canton Uri. All these acts of union cleared the ground for what was soon to be an actual League.

At Grütli, a secluded field below the Seelisberg, in Canton Uri, thirty herdsmen, stout of heart and strong of limb, were brought in 1307 by three good patriots—Werner Stauffacher of Canton Schwyz, Walter Fürst of Canton Uri, and Erni of Melchthal, Canton Unterwalden—to engage each other, by the pledge of 'All for each and each for all.' They swore to rise against their tyrant, to destroy his castles, and to free their Cantons from the Austrian yoke. As Schwyz became the theatre of war, the world outside first heard of these confederates as the Switzers. When Morgarten made the name and flag of Schwyz illustrious, the other Cantons were not sorry to accept her name and banner for their infant League.

Both name and banner are of unknown origin. The name of Schwyz has been derived from swine, from snow, and many other words. The flag was once a blood-red field; the cross was won in fight, but whether in defence of Pope or Kaiser is a subject of dispute. The better story seems, that certain men of Schwyz went out to serve the Emperor Conrad in his wars. They bore with them a blood-red flag. In every fray that blood-red flag was seen in front, and Conrad watched it with a soldier's eye. When the imperial armies moved on Burgundy, these troops marched with them; and in one of the assaults of Héricourt they roused his martial admiration to so high a pitch, that he bestowed on them the right to quarter on their blood-red field his own imperial arms—the pure white cross.

Morgarten fought and won, the herdsmen met in Brunnen, and renewed, in 1315, the League already sworn by them eight years before. In 1332 Luzern became a member; and in 1351 Zürich joined them, bringing in her train the neighbouring towns of Zug and Glarus. Two years later this confederacy was joined by Bern. For upwards of a century and a quarter (1353-1481) these eight Cantons—Zürich, Bern, Luzern, Uri, Schwyz, Unterwalden, Glarus, Zug—composed the League; but in this century and a quarter, Sempach, Näfels, Grandson, Morat, gave the simple mountaineers a taste for war. They broke into Aargau, Thurgau, and Ticino, and annexed these countries to the League, but not as members of a free and equal commonwealth. The conquerors were all but nobles, and the conquered race were all but serfs.

In 1481 they took in Fribourg and Solothurn, as ninth and tenth Cantons. Afterwards they occupied St. Gallen by a Federal force. In 1501 Basel and Schaffhausen were admitted, as eleventh and twelfth Cantons; and a dozen years later Appenzell, a portion of the occupied country of St. Gallen, was accepted as the thirteenth Canton. For upwards of two centuries and three quarters (1513–1798) these thirteen Cantons formed the League.

As yet these Leaguers had no fundamental pact. Each Canton kept her sovereign rights in full; made peace and war, coined money, sent her ministers to king and pope, and exercised the faculties of life and death. She only joined her sisters when their common frontiers were assailed. The Leaguers had no code, no capital, no executive power. When conferences were needed, they were called at either Bern, Luzern, or Zürich; but the deputies conferred, decided, and returned; each man to get his Canton to accept what they had done.

In fact, the League was nothing but a group of states connected by a treaty of alliance, and the name of Switzer nothing but a form of speech occasionally heard in foreign camps.

The actual origin of the League, as now existing, must be traced to France.

In 1798 the French, as friends of liberty, broke into Switzerland, upset the Cantonal governments, and framed a new republic on the last French pattern, one and indivisible. They took away the national name and flag. The countries of the League became Helvetia, and her flag three stripes of yellow, green, and red. They took away the primary assemblies. In their zeal for uniformity, they split some Cantons into pieces, and they patched up several Cantons into one. Bern was divided into four Cantons—Bern, Aargau, Oberland, and Vaud. Ticino parted into Canton Lugano and Canton Bellinzona. Fribourg became Canton Sarine-et-Broye. The two Appenzells were swept away in favour of Canton Sentis. Glarus was lost in Canton De la Linth. Zug, Uri, Schwyz, and Unterwalden, were abolished at one stroke; and Canton Waldstätten occupied their places on the map. They introduced a fundamental pact, a common code of laws, a tree of liberty, and a French directorate of police. No student, mapping out ideal commonwealths, can fail to see how logical these new arrangements were. As a reward for setting up this new republic, one and indivisible in name, and equal in her several parts, the friends of freedom seized Geneva and Neufchatel.

But an ungrateful people rose against these friends of liberty, and after blood was shed in twenty fights, the French renounced the task, so difficult for them, of teaching men who had been free five hundred years, the art of managing their own affairs according to their actual wants. These old republicans could not be taught the beauties of a new republic one and indivisible. The Bernese people burnt their tree of liberty; the citizens of Glarus would not take the name of Linthers; Zug and Uri could not act in union; and the men of Schwyz would not replace their ancient flag. 'Leave them alone,' Napoleon said; and they were henceforth left alone.

In 1803 the modern League was formed. Old names, old banners, and old peasant parliaments, were all restored, and districts which had long been held as subject lands were taken in as members of the League. St. Gallen, Aargau,

Thurgau, Ticino, Vaud, were now accepted as free Cantons, and became the equals of Luzern and Bern. The three republics of the Upper Rhine country were admitted as a fifteenth Canton, with the name of Graubünden. For his services in this affair Napoleon seized the Valais, which he occupied and annexed to France!

In 1814, on the fall of France, the Valais was united to the League; Neufchatel and Geneva also; the last-named Canton much enlarged in size by the addition of Carouge.

The order, names, and dates, stand thus:—

1.	Zürich	. . 1351	12.	Schaffhausen	. 1501
2.	Bern	. . 1353	13.	Appenzell	. 1573
3.	Luzern	. . 1332	14.	St. Gallen	. 1803
4.	Uri .	. . 1307	15.	Graubünden	. 1803
5.	Schwyz	. . 1307	16.	Aargau	. 1803
6.	Unterwalden	. 1307	17.	Thurgau	. 1803
7.	Glarus	. . 1352	18.	Ticino	. 1803
8.	Zug .	. . 1352	19.	Vaud	. 1803
9.	Fribourg .	. 1481	20.	Valais	. 1814
10.	Solothurn	. 1481	21.	Neufchatel	. 1814
11.	Basel	. . 1501	22.	Geneva	. 1814

To find a capital for these republics was no easy task. Each Canton has a capital of her own — the centre of her public life — but no great city overtops the rest, and draws them into moving round her by her mass and weight.

By flux of speech some tiny towns are dignified as cities, such as Sion, with four thousand souls; as Chur, with seven thousand five hundred souls; and Fribourg, with ten thousand souls. Even Bern and Zürich would be tenth-rate towns in England and America. Geneva is the largest town in Switzerland, with forty-two thousand souls. The second town is Basel, of the size of Birkenhead. With all her glories, Zürich is but half the size of Coventry. In truth, this country is a commonwealth of hamlets, not of towns.

When Canton Zürich joined the League, her only rival was Luzern. Luzern was on the forest lake, accessible from every part, while Altdorf, Schwyz and Stanz lie inland from the water's edge. Luzern was walled and safe, and therefore fit to be a capital of the League. But Zürich was a larger city, with a richer trade, a stronger wall, and a more energetic people. She became the centre of activity, though not the seat of government. When Canton Bern came in, the city of that name was sometimes used for conference. Luzern was also used; and thus, from ancient times, three cities of the League acquired the rank, if not the name, of capitals. The League, reformed in 1814, adopted these three cities as her seats of government; the President and Chamber sitting in each Canton for a couple of years, and then migrating to the next in turn. This system lasted from the year 1814 till the war of 1847, when, taught by serious trials that a country must possess one centre, and one centre only, Zürich and Luzern gave up their claims, and Bern became a fixed and central capital of the League.

CHAPTER XVII.

THE FEDERAL PACT.

ALTHOUGH this League of Cantons has survived a hundred monarchies, and never ceased to be a union of republics, she has lived through many forms in her five hundred and seventy-five years of public life. She has been feudal, clerical, imperial, radical, by turns. So long as she has had a Federal Pact, the business of her public life has been to study and amend that Pact. Old men can recollect the constitutions overthrown in 1798; the constitutions overthrown in 1803; the constitutions overthrown in 1814. Young men remember the constitutions broken through in 1846; the new constitutions of 1848; the revision of 1866. All these amendments of the Federal Pact are to be taken as the signs of life and growth. In every stage of her historical growth, the League has been in arms against the Cantons and the

Communes on behalf of general rights; those interests of a citizen, which lie beyond the proper sphere of local laws and customs. With the League are lodged the first conceptions of a Switzer and a Switzerland. In Zürich there are only Zürichers, in Geneva there are only Genevese. A Cantonal code knows nothing of a Switzer and a Switzerland outside; and hence the League is charged with the great duty of converting her conceptions of a Swiss citizen and a Swiss Commonwealth into actual facts.

A man may have some rights beyond the limits of his Canton and his Commune; and a man may lose his claim to call on either Canton or Commune to protect him in his rights.

A Switzer is supposed to be a member of some Commune, in which he is to live and die. Till lately, nineteen out of twenty Switzers followed this old rule, and never left the hamlets of their birth. That system is extremely favourable to simplicity, to permanence, to inter-marriage, and to cretinism; but in the face of opening roads, with steamers on the lakes and tunnels through the alps, it is not easy to maintain this patriarchal system. Men will rove in search of fortune; and by roving they will lose their Communal rights.

But loss of Communal rights will not deter a man from seeking bread beyond his village; and of recent years a movement has been noted by observers which, if quickened in the coming years, must part the population into two great camps—the citizens with Communal rights and the citizens without Communal rights. Already the proportion of citizens who have no Communal rights is great; as some think perilously great; for these men are a class apart, who have no common interest with their fellows, and know no other country than the League. For them the League is fighting, and has always fought. It claims for them the name of Switzer, and a right to settle, with a clear and equal vote, in any part of Switzerland—as they can do in Canton Zürich, under the new and pure republican law.

A man is supposed to marry in his Commune; but a stranger has no right of Commune; and a citizen with Communal rights may wish to take a wife elsewhere. The case of Aloïs Arnold is a common case. Here comes a conflict of the courts. A stranger's marriage may be either good or bad, according to the local law. Some Cantons use the civil form, while others use the clerical form. The Catholic Cantons, as a rule, consider civil

M

marriage as no other than concubinage; and persons living under such a union as no better than adulterers. In such Cantons divorce is not allowed, and marriages of persons who have been divorced in other Cantons are declared illegal and immoral. On the other side, a member of a Commune cannot take a wife unless his mayor and council give him leave; and if he marries in another Canton, these authorities of his village may assoil the honour of his wife, and rob his children of their birthright in the soil. Confusion in his dearest interests wounds the citizen, and scandals irritate the courts of law. A woman who is recognised in Bern as an honourable wife may be rejected by society in Stanz and Altdorf as a concubine. For man and wife in such a case the League is fighting, and has always fought. It claims for them the right to marry when and where they please, without consulting either village priest or parish mayor.

A man is bound to join the standard of his district, and receive his drill and training with his neighbour; but experience proves that since the military art acquired so high a form, it is not wise to leave this drill and training to the several Cantons, some of which neglect their work, while others do that work extremely well. A better method is required; and as the public safety is the highest law, the League desires to place the drill and training of all citizens on a common plan, and under the direction of a single board.

Evangelical and Teutonic Switzerland is bent on having a general law on settlement, on civil marriage, and on military training. Catholic and Teutonic Switzerland is not so warm about these rights; some Cantons stand aloof, and some oppose the project of reform. In Celtic Switzerland the flame of opposition burns at fervent heat. Vaud does not like revision of the pact. Her Communal properties are vast, and she imagines that revision will compel her to admit the Bernese settlers, who are very numerous in her hamlets, to a share in all these village gifts. But Valais takes the lead in opposition; Valais, which has set up gaming-tables; Valais, which is always asking alms in Bern. This Canton feels that she has everything to lose by giving up her Cantonal and Communal rights. Ticino is too languid for resistance; but she does not yield her privilege of incapacity with grace. The Appenzells and Unterwaldens want to walk their ancient ways.

At present there is no great fear of violent

change; but the revision will be made in favour of the citizen and the League. All changes in the Pact—except when France bestowed on Switzerland a new republic—have been guided by historical lights; yet, every change from 1814 down to 1871, has taken something from the Commune and the Canton, and bestowed it on the citizen and the League.

The Pact is written in three chapters. One chapter treats of Political Principles; a second chapter treats of Public Authorities; and a third chapter treats of the Revising Powers.

In Chapter I. these general principles are laid down:

The twenty-two sovereign Cantons form the Swiss League. Their objects are—to defend the country, to maintain peace and order, to protect rights and liberties, and promote the common good. All Switzers are equal before the laws. No Canton is allowed to form political alliances with other Cantons and with foreign states. A power to make treaties and to declare war is lodged with the Federal authorities; but the League is not allowed to keep a standing army. Every Switzer is a soldier, armed and drilled, and when the Council call him, he is bound to serve.

Each Canton furnishes her tale of men; a first line called Elite, a second called Reserve, a third called Landwehr. In the field, a Federal corps must have the national flag. The League collects all customs at the frontier, coins all monies, regulates all railways, telegraphs, and posts. Letters may not be opened. A man can exercise political rights in no more than one Canton. Free exercise of religion is guaranteed. The press is free. The right of petition is admitted. Citizens may form associations, so long as there is nothing dangerous to the state in either the ends pursued or the means employed. Death penalties for political crime are abolished. The League can expel foreigners who compromise the public safety. Jesuits, and societies affiliated to the Jesuits, cannot be received in any part of Switzerland.

In Chapter II. these general rules are given:

Supreme authority is in the Federal Assembly. This Assembly is composed of two sections (like the American House of Representatives and Senate) called the National Council and the Council of States. Apart, each section has a power defined by law; together, they are sovereign, and their acts beyond appeal. They vote without instructions from their clients; they are representatives in the highest sense. Each section chooses its own president and vice-president; and when they sit together, they elect the Federal president, the Federal council, the Federal judges, the Federal chancellor, the Federal representatives, the Federal general, and the Federal chief-of-staff. They make war and peace. They pass laws. Subject to a popular veto, they revise the fundamental pact. The number of the National Council varies; every twenty thousand souls in the population having a right to send one member; that of the Council of States is fixed at forty-four; each Canton sending two members, each Half-canton one member, to the board. All representatives are paid; in one house from the Federal funds, and in the other from the Cantonal funds. A right of voting for his member vests in every Switzer twenty years of age; a right of serving as such member vests in every Switzer who is not a pastor, priest, or monk. Executive power is lodged in a Féderal Council of seven members, named for three years by the Federal Assembly in a common sitting. Any Switzer eligible for the National Council may be chosen as a Federal councillor, whether he is an ordinary councillor or not. The President is named for a single year, and cannot occupy his séat a second year. These Federal councillors are paid ; they must not follow any other calling while they serve the League.

In Chapter III. these powers are taken :

The Federal constitution can be revised at any time. Revision must take place according to the legal forms. If either branch of the Federal Assembly should propose revision, and the other branch refuse, thè question must be put to popular vote. If fifty thousand Switzers, having civil rights, demand revision, and the Chamber will not yield, the question must' be also put to popular vote. A clear majority decides the matter. When a constitution is revised by the National Assembly, it must be submitted to the people for their sanction, and will have no force until accepted by a clear majority of citizens, voting man by man, and also by a clear majority of Cantons voting state by state.

There is scant need to say that such a system gives an influence to the smaller Cantons in excess of their natural and financial force. This power comes down to them from ancient times, and in the hour of scientific justice (such as that of 1798) it would be swept away. In all political struggles Uri counts as much as Bern, and Zürich finds her vote annulled by that of Zug.

These minor States are Catholic, and many of their people Ultramontane. As the battle of the moment rages round the Catholic standards mainly—as the purpose of the Liberal party is to back the League against the Catholic Cantons—as the object of revision is to break the spell now exercised by priests and Jesuits over schoolroom, camp, and council, in these tiny Cantons—every soldier of the church is up in arms against revision of the fundamental pact. Once more the Jesuits are astir. Once more a pilgrimage is preached. Once more the pulpits breathe the note of strife. A memoir on the Catholic case against the Liberal party is prepared by Gaspard Mermillod. The Band of Pio Nono, a society of pious souls, is called to witness for the truth. All Switzerland is agitated by the church.

CHAPTER XVIII.

JESUITS.

'THEY cannot take away our right of speech,' a Jesuit says, his pale, meek face aglow with inner light, as we descend into the streets of Fribourg, where a gathering of the Catholic party has been called.

Although the Jesuits as an Order, with their schools and churches, with their presence and supremacy, are not allowed by law to root themselves in any Canton of the League, the members of this Order come and go like any other strangers, whether Jews or Turks; and in the passing year —a time of trial for their church—they swarm in every town, from Basel to Lugano. They are watching the Old Catholic movements; they are wrestling with the Radical papers; they are egging on the Cantons to resist the introduction of civil marriage; they are fighting for the spiritual powers against the civil powers; they are contending for amendments in the fundamental pact; and they are holding up to public sympathy the image of a persecuted and infallible Pope.

'These men can seize our goods,' the Father adds; 'can strip us of our right to teach; can turn our convents into mills and barracks; can expel us from our native land. They hold the sword, at present; yet, with all their might, they cannot hinder us from meeting to petition, and from interceding with the saints.'

'But are not many of your opponents Catholic?'

'Not one. They are not Christian. Nay, they curse that noble name, as Satan and his angels curse it in their flaming pit. Five years ago they struck the name of Christian from two articles in the fundamental pact. They left it in one article; and now they are erasing it from that. If they could burn the churches and behead the priests, they would. All churches will be taken in their turn—the first, that Church which stands upon a living rock.'

This gathering of the church is called, in name, to celebrate the founding of the Band of Pio Nono, but in truth to rouse the public mind against the fundamental pact. The Band of Pio Nono is a league of pious souls, who wish to help the Pope with pence, to scatter tracts about the villages, and work against the Liberal press. Herr Theodor von Scherrer is the president of this body; but the Jesuits who have called this meeting have another end in view.

The Jesuits love this city on the Sarine; first, because it is their ancient seat; and next, because it is a town in which the age and people of the crusades still exist. Luzern, the other Jesuitic capital of Switzerland, has been invaded by the stranger, and has learned to care for money, bridges, banks, and public gardens, more than for this ancient Order, and the church they serve. The wayside cross is disappearing from her streets. A railway-engine drowns her vesper-bell. No beggars wait for pottage at her convent-doors. Few men now doff their caps to priest and nun. No crowds of women follow the viaticum with downcast eyes and quivering lips. A Catholic Council, it is true, still occupies the Rathhaus; but a Catholic Council in Luzern is not so pliant as this Order likes. Luzern has grown too fat for a submissive town. The grace of poverty has left her; and her lines of chestnut-avenues, steamboat piers, and new hotels, rise up in evidence against the latest gospels brought by them from Rome. Some warning reaches them from day to day. Eugène, Bishop of Basel, asks Professor Herzog, of the seminary of Luzern, to make a public declaration of the Pope's Infallibility. Eugène's diocese extends beyond Luzern, and Herzog, therefore, is canonically subject to him. What is the result? Herr Segesser, though a Catholic, gives notice to the State Council of a motion to protest against the interference of a Catholic prelate with the duties of a Catholic priest! In Fribourg there is no such spirit. Since the Jesuits came to dwell in Fribourg, now three centuries ago, the town has been their own. When all the world made war upon them, Fribourg was their refuge and defence. She was the last to send them out; she was the first to call them back. In 1847 she fought for them, and had her children slain for them. Driven out again, suppressed by law, and banished as an Order from Swiss soil, she still regards them as a band of martyrs, keeps their convent on this height untouched, and longs to see them back in their old place, if only she might have them back without a civil war. She is not game enough to fight. But as to voting, listening, lighting lamps, and burning Bengal fire for them, she will go any lengths. Etienne Marilley, Bishop of Lausanne, whose see extends to Fribourg, is a man of vigour—silent, humorous, circumspect—who keeps his house in order and his flock in trim. This bishop may be said to rule the town, since no man can be either mayor or councillor till Etienne nods assent. The government is ultramontane. All the officers of state are members of the Band of Pio Nono. Priests are made inspectors of the public schools. An order of nuns, the Ursulines, affiliated to the Jesuits, and directed by a Jesuit father, is received into the city in defiance of the fundamental law. No strangers come to live in Fribourg. When the bridge is crossed, the organ heard, the Jesuits' convent seen, the Rathhaus visited, a traveller hurries on to Bern. Few strangers rest beyond a night; one good hotel suffices for their wants. No roads are made, no avenues planted, to entice them; and in many parts the city keeps a something of that quaint and feudal aspect which it wore when Louis of

Savoy dashed into the Rathhaus, seized the thirteen German patriots, and struck their heads off in the Place Saint George.

Two thousand deputies, at least, have answered to the Jesuits' bidding; come to dine and listen, since they dare not draw the sword. They make no secret of their mood, for Switzers are not silent when their hearts are full. Their voices are for war. 'The time has come,' exclaims the chancellor of Solothurn, 'when we must preach a crusade!' Here, he holds his breath an instant, for the word upon his lip means civil strife; and then adds, slowly, 'Not an armed crusade; arms are not within our reach; but in its stead a crusade of the Cross.'

This crusade has begun. A Capuchin monk, one Father Hilaire, is our Peter Hermit. Tall, ascetic, furious, he attracts all eyes and takes all ears by storm. Attacking modern progress in general, and the Old Catholic party in particular, he exclaims—'First liberty, then liberalism, then license. There is a Pagan liberalism; there is also an heretical liberalism; and there is also a Catholic liberalism. This last is worse than all the rest. The Holy Father has pronounced it dangerous to the souls of men. What does it mean? Luther is the father of modern liberalism and modern impiety, and one of his disciples, Guizot, has the folly to declare that the church should only speak to heart and mind, and not appeal to actual force. I tell you that the state is a father, and a father knows that he must use the rod. These liberals prate of kindness and persuasion, but the Holy Scriptures tell us not to spare. St. Francis got a whipping for his fault : it was his first fault and his last. The state must use, not arguments, but whips. Stand fast, I bid you, to the church : you have the truth ; and truth will make you free.'

At a dinner given to the Swiss bishops in the Mercers' tavern, near the church of St. Nicolas, this picture of a militant church is touched by more than one episcopal orator. 'No one,' says Etienne Marilley, leading off replies to a toast of 'The Swiss Prelates,' 'can equal your bishops in desire to stand by their several flocks in this conflict ; and if it should become necessary to throw themselves into the breach, and pay with life for their devotion to the cause of truth and justice, your bishop will be the first to do it.' Shouts of rapture greet this note of coming war. Marilley pauses ; something seems to strike him; something perhaps of comic in this tavern boast of readiness to die; and turning to his reverend brother, Gaspard Mermillod, he adds: 'Now *he* shall speak: you know how eloquent he is; his tongue is looser than my own—il a la langue mieux pendu que moi.'

Bishop Mermillod takes up the martial tone, —'Your bishops give no half support to any cause in which they are engaged; you may rely upon their watchfulness and courage in this coming shock of foes. Remember who commands us in the hour of strife. Our General-in-chief is the Holy Father; but in battle, every soldier must be at his post, and no less credit falls upon the rank and file than on the captains. Fribourg, which has borne so long her witness for the truth, now leads the van. Inspired by her, Luzern will join our ranks, and then the whole of Catholic Switzerland will rally to the church.' Abbot Wicky springs upon his feet to give a toast of 'War—a holy war!' His face is flushed and red, his words rush from him fast and fierce. 'Our Lord has told us He brought war into the world. St. Paul could boast that he had fought the good fight. Indifference will not do. If any one of my flock were to neglect his duty at the polling-booth, I would refuse to grant him absolution from his sins. No, no; this day is not a time to talk of peace. I give my toast, A war— a holy war.' In place more fitting for a bishop to be heard in than a tavern, Mermillod still sounds the clarion. 'When we are gone,' he cries, in one of his great bursts of eloquence, that almost sets the college close on fire, 'impartial history will paint four figures on the canvas of our time; four figures, standing out distinct in form and high in light, amidst the gloomy shadows of the past; a kaiser leaning on a cannon at Versailles, an emperor yielding up his sword at Sedan, a soldier-king caressing his moustache and riding into Rome; and over these three figures, blessing them with lifted hands, the calm, majestic figure of Pius the Ninth, committing a renewed and happy kingdom of the church to his successor Pius the Tenth.'

At night, the city is aflame with lamps. The bridge, the Place St. George, the streets and terraces, are crowded with excited priests not dining at the Mercers' tavern. On the Schönberg stands a cross of coloured lamps. The chapel of Loretto is a wreath of stars, with Pio Nono in the centre, writ in fire. At Diessbach there are rockets, Bengal lights, and detonating balls. Some strangers, lingering on the terrace of the Zähringer Hof, make witty and annoying jokes about this pious crusade; but by ten o'clock, these revellers have gone to bed; and we are left with the autumnal stars and silent city, to compare opinions on a warm day's work.

'You hope to influence the revision by these meetings?'

'Yes,' replies the Jesuit, 'we may hope to do so; but our trust is not in deputies and lawyers; else these jesters who have left us would be wholly in the right. Our trust is in the higher powers. You recollect the state of things a few years after our great founder's death. We came to Canton Fribourg, to revive and to restore our faith. We had a cruel fight, but we endured and won. Once more, we shall endure and win; but we shall not address the jurists and the doctors; they are useless to us, even when we win them; and we never win them to our side till we have won their masters.'

'Masters!—who are they?'

'The people,—those who delve and drive, who weave and spin, who plough and plant; the porters, shepherds, masons, drovers, boatmen, foresters, and guides. These are the men we seek; for it is only through such men that changes in the world are made. A few days hence, a separate meeting of these classes will be called in Fribourg, in the name of Cantonal sovereignty and freedom of instruction, to protest against revision of the fundamental pact in any other than a strictly Catholic sense. This meeting will protest against the Federals sending any man —at any time, and under any pretext—to report upon a Catholic school. They will protest against a law for closing public schools to priests and nuns. They will protest against the cry for separating church and state. They will demand three great concessions from the League :—the first, that Catholic parents shall have the free choice of teachers for their boys and girls; the second, that every Commune shall have the right to send her children to religious schools; the third, that instead of separating church and state there shall be a closer bond of school and church, teacher and priest, grammar and catechism, science and God. Our people have a right to ask for such things; and when people in this country ask in earnest, they can hardly be denied.'

'But something more than this demand for

freedom of instruction lies behind? You are expecting to return?'

'We ask that restoration as our right. We do not seek a privilege for ourselves; we ask that all religious bodies, known and authorised by the Catholic church, be tolerated and received in Switzerland, like other corporations. We believe in prayer. The church is passing through a bitter time; but as the clouds grow darker, we shall brace our sinews up to meet the storm. We call upon the Virgin day and night. We go on pilgrimage, and seek for courage at Our Lady's shrine.'

CHAPTER XIX.

PILGRIMAGE.

On pilgrimage! Alert but dusty, we attain the chapel called the Ecce Homo, where the path from Goldau through the pine-trees strikes the road from Schwyz to Rothenthurm. A priest from Bellinzona and myself are wending by those bridle-ways that pilgrims love, towards Meinrad's Cell. This chapel gained, the priest kneels down before the cross to say his prayers.

St. Meinrad is a name in the poetic roll of saints, and idlers hear of him, and of his cell, in many a song and play. His shrine was famous at an early time:—

> Von allen Wandiern am dem deutschen Land
> Die über Meinrad's zell . . .

Yet we are not going up this dusty road for Schiller's sake. We have a present purpose in our journey; one of us to pray for light and help, the other to observe the force and passion of the strife.

All Christian countries have their sacred places, which to pilgrims not robust enough in faith for greater doings, have to stand for Bethlehem, Nazareth, and the Holy Sepulchre. Italy has Loretto; Greece, Mount Athos; Russia, Solovetsk; Germany, Cologne; Spain, Compostella; France, St. Denis; England, Walsingham; selected places, owned and blessed of God, in which a sinner, groaning under weight of sin, may spend some moments of his life with holy men and in the midst of holy things. At Meinrad's Cell—Einsiedeln, Anchorite's seat—a pious Switzer finds a spot like one of these; a spot which God has marked and sanctified; a spot of supernatural light and grace, with sacred forests and miraculous waters; in the midst of which the Virgin and her Son have deigned to build their house and consecrate their holy spring.

A noisy beck, the Aa, is at our feet, deep down among the stones and pines. Beyond this ravine springs the Mostelberg. It is a classic and historic scene, alive with noble names and noble deeds. Below is Steinen, where the old Landammann,

Werner Stauffacher, lived; a little lower still is Schwyz; the capital of Canton Schwyz, with her twin prongs of rock. Above are Sattel, with the chapel of Morgarten, and the ridges of that famous alp. To right and left, in front and rear, each crest and thorpe recalls some memorable name and day.

'You call this country free,' the priest observes, on rising from before that wayside cross. 'Although a Switzer born and bred, I am not free to say my prayers in Switzerland's most favoured church! The fact is so. Our Rádicals in Ticino have decreed that no one shall go out on pilgrimage beyond his Canton. I am forced to break that law in going on my duty to Einsiedeln. It is only on our flag we bear the Cross.'

This priest is young and fierce; his southern blood inflamed by what he calls his personal wrong. By law, as he contends, he is the parish priest of B——, a village near Locarno, blest to his appointment by his bishop, but expelled alike from church and commune by a Radical mayor, supported by a squad of Cantonal troops.

'These Radicals not only check our right of pilgrimage, but in a month or two will strike the name of Christian from our public code.'

'But such erasure is no consequence of Radical opinions. Look at Zürich. There the Radicals are masters of the Canton; they have made a new republic; but they have not separated church and state, and have not struck the name of Christian from their public code.'

'In Zürich the majority are Evangelical, and for the passing moment Radicals and Evangelicals fancy they have found a common enemy in Rome. Yet even in Zürich, as in Aargau and in Thurgau, they have seized our convents and our convent-funds.'

'By regular course of law.'

'No course is regular that robs the Church. These injuries are done in face of the most solemn public acts. Our ancient constitutions guaranteed our convents in the mixed Cantons, such as Zürich, Bern, and Basel. In the constitutions of 1803 and 1815 our convents were protected by the League. In 1848 these guarantees were dropped; but not with our consent; and since that dreadful year, our convents, abbeys, and foundations, have been made the prey of Radical and Evangelical majorities in every market-town. You call that regular course of law—the passion of a rude and guilty mob! To us, majorities are not divine.'

'Are not the men who carry on these conflicts with the church of Rome, her children, men like Keller, Landammann of Aargau, Curti, Landammann of St. Gallen, President Anderwert of Thurgau, and Professor Münzinger of Bern?'

'Our children sin through ignorance. They think the church an enemy to their civic freedom; she who is their steadfast friend. They never dream how much our country owes the church. Our goods, our laws, our towns, our liberties—all these are of her friendly gift. We had our church before we had a Commune; we had our Commune ere we had a Canton; we had our Cantons long before we had a League. What would you call the glories of our land?'

'Zürich, Luzern, Geneva, and St. Gallen.'

'You are right; and all these towns are offshoots from the church.'

No man can say the priest is wrong, and many of these pilgrims toiling up the cliffs towards Meinrad's Cell, preserve traditions in their songs and usages of old dependence on the cloister. Zürich lived in her Lady-abbesses. Luzern depended on the Abbots of Murbach. Geneva was indebted to her bishops; and St. Gallen owed her name to a famous saint. The pasture-lands were occupied by nuns, the alpine tops were tenanted by monks. From Basel to Sion, nearly every town of moment was the property of some great abbey, chapter and cathedral. Sion held of her bishop; St. Maurice of her abbot. Solothurn depended on the chapter of St. Ursus Münster; and Schaffhausen on the abbots of All Saints. The nuns of Zürich planted Uri, and the monks of Murbach planted Unter-walden. Even Schwyz, though many of her people were free peasants of the empire, was a sort of appanage of the church. Large tracts of Schwyz were claimed by the Prince-abbot of Einsiedeln; though the men of Schwyz refused his rents, and when he used the weapons of his cloth against them rushed upon his convent, stole his cattle, and profaned his shrine.

'The world is arming more and more against the Church,' the Father from Ticino adds; 'yet since the day of Pentecost, the world has never stood in greater need than now of spiritual grace. It may not come, though hearts are straining for an outward sign. You see these children of the soil; these aged men, who look to find their graves ere long; these boys and girls, with brows unseamed by care; these young men and young women, in the pride of health; the men of every grade, from priest and banker down to groom and guide; the women of all ranks, from nun and teacher down to kitchen wench and nurse. All these are going up to Meinrad's cell. But who is Meinrad, that these folks should care for him? What brings them from their distant homes? What lifts them over pass and lake? Who bids them slake their thirst at Meinrad's fountain? You can count them now by scores; at Biberbrücke they will swell to hundreds; in the convent square they will expand to thousands. Why are they afoot? No earthly purpose draws them up into these wastes. No church is to be robbed, no Jesuit to be hunted down. No popular parliament is to be held. Yet nowhere in these Cantons will you match the concourse of all classes at Our Lady's shrine. Why have this rustic and his wife come down from Andermatt, a hundred miles of mountain road on foot? To eat and drink, to lodge in dainty rooms, to spend a joyous and mercurial day? They dream of no such pleasures. They are coming on the soul's affairs. Not meat and wine, but grace and light, are what they seek. In asking for a blessing, they are quickened by an impulse more than human to go out and find it in some holy place. If tender and poetic fancies haunt their dreams, these longings are a spiritual, not a mortal growth. They seek for peace, and they will find it in the house of God.'

The passing season is a Pilgrim's Year. In every season there are crowds of devotees at Meinrad's Cell; but never has the church been tried as now; and never has Our Lady's shrine been thronged as now. In every town the Jesuits, and the ultramontane priests who back them, have been preaching pilgrimage. All sacred enterprises open with a visit to some saint. A pilgrimage prepares the mind to dare and suffer. All the deputies who troop to Rome, both clerical and lay, are counselled by the Jesuits to return from Italy by way of Canton Schwyz. All through the summer and the fall, a stream of English lords, of Belgian counts, and Austrian barons, have been dropping cards on Abbot Heinrich Schmid, and kneeling at the hour of vespers in Our Lady's shrine.

'These pilgrimages serve a worldly and political end?'

'In one sense — yes. We seek a change. We cannot bear the pressure of events. Take my own Canton of Ticino. By our fundamental law the Roman Catholic and Apostolic Church is recognised as teaching the religion of the state; yet see what they are doing in the face of that undoubted public law. Our radicals have seized the Catholic colleges at Ascona, Mendrisio, Bellinzona, and Lugano. They have interrupted the education of our priests; they have driven away our vicars from their churches; they have robbed our bishop of his rights; they have suppressed the seminary of Polleggio; they have set up excommunicated priests. They laugh at protests from our spiritual chief, and interdict his visits to the churches on our soil.'

'He is a foreign prelate, is he not — the Bishop of Milan — and a subject of the King of Italy?'

'A bishop — yes; a subject — no. He is a shepherd of the Universal Church, which sees no frontier lines in Christian states.'

'But is there not a law — a Federal law of 1859 — which interdicts, in every part of Switzerland, the exercise of episcopal jurisdiction by any foreign bishop?'

'Yes; there is a law; and that bad law is but another of our wrongs. Those Radicals in Bern are like our Radicals in Ticino. First, they rob the Church, and then they pass a bill to make their plunder lawful spoil. Our Council in Ticino were before the men of Bern. They made a law, in 1855, by which they took away our bishop's right to choose his priests and vicars. They bade some six or seven laymen, ignorant of the service, to conduct our Church affairs; to do as they might choose with hospices and convents; to appoint ecclesiastical dignitaries; to install our clergy in their charges; to erect new parishes where they liked, and even to suppress old parishes according to their mood. Nay, more; they gave the mayors and councils—shepherds, porters, grooms—a right to send away their village priests, and set up others in their seats. It is rebellion in the church. The bishop and the Pope are equally defied. In future, every act and edict of the spiritual powers are to be laid before the Canton for approval; if approval is refused, such acts and edicts are to have no force. A priest is bound to read in church all edicts of the civil powers. If any priest should act on orders sent to him from either Rome or Milan, he is smitten by a fine, which may be five francs, fifty francs, five thousand francs. What man dare do his duty to his bishop under such a threat? Some persons try to keep their conscience clear; but if they rise against the excommunicated priests set up in divers places by the state, a bugle sounds to arms, the troops are set in motion, and the rifle stops all argument with a bang.'

'Ticino, though a Catholic Canton, seems to be in plain revolt against her Church?'

'It is in actual schism. Our bishop dares not come into his diocese. Our celebration of the month of Mary is prohibited. A woman is condemned and fined for singing the Canticles of the Virgin. Our wish to celebrate the Papal jubilee is refused. A pilgrimage to any shrine beyond the Canton is forbidden, so that no man from Ticino can, according to his local law, be now upon his way to Meinrad's Cell. Is it not clear that we require a change of heart and soul? To bring about this change of heart and soul, we preach the Pilgrim's Year.

CHAPTER XX.

CONVENT AND CANTON.

At the small village of Altmatt, which was once the border town of Canton Schwyz, defended by some earthworks from attacks by the Prince-abbot of Einsiedeln, and is now a little weaving thorpe, we quit the road and climb the mountain side. A pilgrim always keeps the ancient tracks, and this old pathway up the Katzenstrick was worn in ages long ago by knights and shepherds in their frequent raids and frays.

An hour of easy idling brings us up from Altmatt to the top; a table-land of green and lonely pastures, where the Convent herds were wont to feed. Behind us rise the broken and irregular ridges of Morgarten; name as sacred to a Switzer as Mount Zion to a Jew.

'You may imagine,' says the priest, on pausing to look backward, 'that the glory of Morgarten springs directly from the oaths of Grütli and the deeds of Tell. We priests are not all Austrian in our passions; and, in spite of Kopp and Rilliet, may agree with every shepherd on these mountain slopes, that Tell was once a living man; but Grütli oath and Altdorf apple have but scant connexion with the day of which some Switzers feel so proud. Morgarten was the fruit of an indecent raid and an atrocious theft. These men of Schwyz are always men of Schwyz. They prate of freedom much, but what they mean by freedom is a right of making free with other people's goods. Their spirit has descended, like their banner, to the League, which only robs our convents now, as in an earlier day this Canton robbed St. Meinrad's Cell.'

In early times the abbots of Einsiedeln, princes of the Empire, held their lands in sovereignty, protected by the church and by some noble knight—the Graf von Rapperschwyl and Duke of Austria mainly; while the men of Schwyz, affecting to be peasants of the empire, would not own the sway of a religious house. All efforts to subdue them only made them worse. No frontiers could be fixed between the Convent and the Canton. They were said to run across these pasture lands along the Katzenstrick, and when the convent cows and horses strayed into disputed fields, the shepherds caught and stole them. Angry words roused angry blood. The abbot claimed the country, and the rustics answered they were free and always had been free.

Frei war der Schweitzer von Uralters her.

They owned no master save that emperor to whom the knee of king and serf alike was bent. The abbots of Einsiedeln, princes of the empire, with the habits of their class, replied that they had charters from the emperor which would prove their claims. The men of Schwyz were not allowed to see these charters, and when they raised a cry against being spoiled, the abbot struck them with a thunder-bolt from Rome.

A year before the battle of Morgarten threw a lurid light into these Swiss defiles, Johannes, Baron von Schwanden, Canton Bern, was reigning abbot; a deceitful, grasping man, who coveted his neighbour's field, and built himself a fortress on the Lake of Zürich, as a refuge from the crowd of enemies whom his crimes raised up. No Austrian bailiff, in his wantonness of power, put out his hand in a more ruthless spirit than this Benedictine prince. He laid the country under interdict; he closed the churches, stopped the rites of baptism and confession, and prohibited the sacraments of marriage and viaticum. When the afflicted people asked by what authority he laid them under interdict, he told them he was acting under briefs from Rome.

The men of Schwyz, excited and indignant, came from mass into their primary assembly at the feast of the Epiphany (1314), to hear the news, and see what could be done. Werner Stauffacher, Landammann of Schwyz, presided at this meeting, and the question rose in what way they could see these Roman briefs and charters which were said to be at Meinrad's Cell. Should they not march upon the abbey, and obtain a sight of them by force? This proposition took the crowd. A raid upon that stronghold of their enemies might pay them well. If it were boldly planned, and quickly done, a raid might yield them more than briefs and charters, even if such briefs and charters should be found. The monks were rich; their stables full of horses, and their pastures fat with kine. These monks were sons of dukes and counts, who made their Benedictine skirts a cloak for every vice. Their castle on the Lake of Zürich stood beyond the reach of simple shepherds, but the abbey of Einsiedeln lay at hand, not three hours' march from Schwyz. Much fiery speech was used, and then a vote was taken for a march that Sunday night. At once they sent off scouts to stop the roads, lest news of what was in the wind should reach the monks. They called each citizen to his flag, and being armed already they were quickly on the march by Rothenthurm and Altmatt towards this Katzenstrick.

Rudolf von Rudegg, Rector of the seminary of Einsiedeln, wrote a poem on this raid of rustics, full of quaint and picturesque details. Rudegg calls his work 'Capella Heremit;' and in the latter part of this quaint piece he paints the night surprise.

'All at once,' he writes, 'in the midst of darkness the convent bell rings out a note of danger; but we are too late to fly; the enemy has posted his men on every side. Each one of us endeavours to leave his cell and gain the sanctuary in the church, which he supposes that even these robbers will respect, but it is only in the upper chamber of the belfry that one feels assured of finding a place of safety. Some of us run among our enemies, who make us prisoners; some resist this capture and are threatened by the mob with instant death. The chief, however, calls his company, and setting them to watch the captive monks, prevents the rogues from going into any more excess.'

This presence of the Landammann might have warned the fathers that the business was more serious than a raid on flocks and herds, had any of these learned nobles known the name of Werner Stauffacher, and the existing temper of the men of Schwyz. But none of these proud monks had stooped as yet to learn the commonest facts about those peasant neighbours who were soon to be the burthen of a hundred songs— the talk of every court and city from the Tiber to the Thames. The Rector had not heard of Werner's name.

So soon as the invaders seized the place, they sought in every room, in every press, for papers. All the books they found were burnt. Accounts and psalters were destroyed in heaps; but the pretended bulls and charters were not found; a fact which Rudegg feels he must explain away by saying that the abbot had bestowed them in some secret chest. This abbot was at Pfäffikon, his fortress on the lake.

'Our Convent,' says the Rector, who was hiding in the belfry, 'is delivered up to pillage. Everything is seized, the sanctuary doors are chopped with hatchets, when the ornaments, the sacred vessels and the priestly robes become the spoil of wretches, who trample under foot and scatter to the winds, not only bones of martyrs but the consecrated bread . . . When daylight comes, the foe draws round the belfry, armed with burning torch and bar of iron, ready to assault and make the fathers yield. The porter of the Convent throws himself into the narrow stair, and tells the fathers he can hold it with his axe, since only one invader can come in at once; but they decline this offer of defence, as not becoming monks, and put themselves into the hands of God. On meeting with no obstacle to their advance, the enemy enter in, but we receive them in the words of peace. "You need not fear," says one of them, "our chief has given us orders only to take your persons and your goods." Happy to know the worst, we follow them without a word. They lodge us in a separate house, which is our jail. But now another band arrives, and finding nothing more to eat and drink, these men grow riotous, and ask to have their share of plunder and of prisoners. Such a row breaks out! At length, the chief calls in his men, and gives his orders for the march. The aged and the sick are left behind.

Three groups are formed; a group of monks, a group of servants, and a group of cattle; and the word to march being given, these columns move, although the women of the village rend the air with screams, and call on Heaven for help, on seeing their husbands driven away with us. In crawling up the Katzenstrick, we all knock up, and I am fain to lie and rest, but that a rider bids me hold on to the tail of his mule. Having crossed the ridge we come down into Altmatt, where we halt. Our Convent servants, at a cost of so much money, are released. For us, we are detained as prisoners in the house of Werner Abacker, where we lie five days, until the Landammann comes to carry us down the road to Schwyz. The monks are made to go on foot. The priests have horses; but our singing-master, dressed in his official costume, cannot get his boots, which are enormous, into the stirrups. So his legs hang down, in which ridiculous way we pass through laughing crowds, into the streets of Schwyz. On stopping at the Communal house, the mayor and councillors dispute what shall be done with us; and during this debate, the curé of Schwyz obtains permission of the Landammann to offer us a good repast. At night, the Landammann comes to tell us we are placed under guard of Peter Jocholf, which alarms us much; this fellow, the wickedest man in the town, has no compassion. Nine of us, seven monks and priests, and two laymen, the Intendant and the porter, are left with him to sup. We sup on tears, and when we rise from table, having eaten nothing, the women, who are far worse than the men, attack us with their cries—"It is too good for them! These monks who have unjustly smitten us with excommunication, and snatched the nurture from our mouths! They ought to suffer as they make us suffer, and to bear the penalties of their misdeeds!" Six weeks they keep us in our narrow jail, and then they take the porter and Intendant to another house. Soon afterwards we beg to send a messenger who may prepare the means of our enlargement, and the Landammann, after speaking with the elders, lets him go. This deputy, Rudolf von Wunnenberg, sees the Graf von Toggenburg and the Graf von Hapsburg, and procures from them two letters of intercession to the Landammann of Schwyz. In three days after Wunnenberg's return, a primary assembly meets; our pardon is pronounced; and we are free once more. The curé, who eleven weeks since had made us sit down at his table to distract our thoughts, now gives us a splendid feast in sign of our joyful deliverance. Having done credit to his meat and wine—his wine is very good!—we start to seek our abbot, who is so much overcome on seeing us alive and safe that tears roll down his cheeks. He serves us up a copious banquet, and he passes round the table ample cups. Thus comforted with meat and wine we let the time slip by with very joyful hearts.'

These monks being men of noble birth, the shame of their imprisonment was widely felt. One captive was a Graf von Regensberg. A second was a follower of the Graf von Hapsburg. Nearly all the monks were knights and barons. Hardly were these noble monks at home before they laid an interdict once more on Canton Schwyz; and called upon the House of Austria to maintain their curse, not only in the land of Schwyz, but in the lands of every one who dared to help it. Austria leaped into the saddle; rode up to Morgarten; and recoiled as from a wall of solid rock.

'Two steps and we shall see St. Meinrad's Cell,' exclaims the priest. We leave the pasture-lands behind, and skirt the edges of a pine-wood.

Down the steep, a little in advance, we see some rustics on their knees, and throwing up their hands in prayer. 'They catch the towers, not yet in sight for us,' the father cries. 'There—there!' and down he sinks upon his knee.

Far out in front extends a green, uneven valley, closed by sombre hills; a bottom rich in grass and water, and of width unusual in these rugged glens. A road winds through the valley, passing many a house and church, till it is lost in a rough nest of sheds and shingles, lying at the feet, though with respect and distance, of a strange and princely pile. This edifice closes up the valley with enormous towers and wings, and looks in solitary grandeur like some fragment of an alpine crest enchanted into sacred forms. This edifice is the Benedictine abbey of Einsiedeln, with the fine basilica of Our Lady of the Anchorites; rising from the gentle hill, which was St. Meinrad's cell and tomb, a convent no less striking in her natural loneliness and visible beauty, than she is in her historic fame and busy daily life.

CHAPTER XXI.

ST. MEINRAD'S CELL.

ST. MEINRAD's Cell has grown into a church, an abbey, and a town.

An open space, like that of the Piazza of San Pietro on a smaller scale, divides the sacred edifice from the town; a wide and windy open space, in which a hundred thousand pilgrims might have room, in one of their great festivals, to kneel before the banner and the cross, as these are carried past them by a line of priests and nuns.

This open square has more than passing hints of Rome. The abbots who conceived the work were princes of the Holy Roman Empire, and the builders kept their faces firmly fixed on Rome. The convent and the church are Romanesque; the esplanade, the statues, and the steps Italian. Everything within them, and about them, has been planned and executed in the Roman spirit. In the centre of this square a fountain drips and sings; a flight of stairs leads up to the basilica; and two arcades of stone sweep round a portion of the front, in modest imitation of Bernini's colonnades.

Much water must be tasted in this public square. The fountain dripping in the centre, called Our Lady's Spring, is said to be a wonder-working source. Einsiedeln is a place of miracles, but greater than all other miracles are those effected at Our Lady's Spring. A statue of the Virgin stands below an open canopy, on seven grey marble shafts, and having on the apex an imperial crown, surmounted by those emblems of her queenly rank—a globe, a crescent, and a star. A wonder-working source, the pilgrims say it is; at which the blind are made to see, the dumb are taught to speak, and perishing souls are purified from sin. A legend runs that once upon a time our Lord himself sat down beside this Virgin's spring, as He in other seasons sat by Jacob's well, and having cooled his lips with pure and copious draughts, rose up and left his blessing on the waters evermore. When first a pilgrim comes into the town, he hurries to this fountain in his search of grace. But here a trouble touches him. Instead of throwing out the water by a single jet, Our Lady's fountain drops it into troughs by fourteen different beaks — the beaks of mystic birds and beasts — in bronze. From which of these bronze beaks our Saviour drank no legend tells. Of fourteen, only one is blessed. To find that one without a guide is hopeless, and the fervent pilgrim, to be sure of drinking from the true one, has to drink from all.

A little of the nectar will not serve. A little washing will not cleanse from sin. The leper had to dip in Jordan several times. Nor is it well to slight so rare a gift. If you are bidden to a feast, you should not wrong your host by merely smiling at his fare. To thank him for his bounty, you must eat. In passing Jacob's well, no pious soul (supposing that the well has water in it) will be satisfied with a sip; nor must the pilgrim at Our Lady's Spring be satisfied with tasting of the sacred jet. He ought to take his draught from every beak, and fourteen draughts of water are enough to quench his thirst, although the day be hot, and he has marched a dozen leagues.

A hundred men and women are about the taps and troughs, each waiting for his turn to drink; the men and women of all countries and all classes, and arrayed in every costume of the civilized earth. An English peeress stands beside a Swabian tramp; a Belgian count is pressing on the toes of an Italian monk. Old soldiers, market-women, stalwart shepherds, sleek and subtle priests, young mothers with their babies at the breast, and hobbling grandsires, blear of eye and weak of arm, are struggling for a place. Some people—mostly women—push their way from beak to beak, all round the fountain, taking each in turn, and therefore certain of the tale; but others have to cut in here and there, from number two to number seven, from number nine to number twelve; and these poor souls are puzzled at the end of a long effort as to whether they have drunk from each and all. If any doubt is on their minds, they must begin afresh.

Yes—here is Sister Agnes in the crowd! Her garb is dustier, and her face more tanned; but in her recognising glance there is a memory of that wayside cross by which she sat, that glacier where she lost her way and fell, that sunset talk from which she turned and fled. She shrinks, no little frightened, from the stout Teutonic dames and lasses, who invade the taps and troughs, and swagging heavy skirts about them, push and shoulder off the weaker fry of pilgrims.

Sister Agnes looks at me and asks,—'Will you not drink—the waters have been blessed?'

'Do you accept this legend of the spring?' I ask a Benedictine father, who has joined us in the square.

'Why not?' exclaims the priest, forestalling what the Benedictine father is about to say; 'in every age, at every corner of this holy place, you find a miracle—a fire put out, a demon exorcised, a battle won by prayer, a pest subdued, a maniac cured, a prisoner released, a shipwrecked sailor saved, an inundation stopped, a withered hand restored, a dumb man taught to speak, a bilious fever cooled, a paralytic healed—then, why not trust a miracle at Our Lady's Spring?'

'It is not written in our books,' the calmer Benedictine father adds. 'We have a list of supernatural graces on our record; they extend through many ages, and these graces have not ended yet, we trust; but in these special acts of providence we find no record of our Saviour's visit to this spring.'

'Your list is incomplete,' the priest exclaims; 'you leave out all your greater miracles; though these are certified by holy men, and recognised as true in Rome. You drop the miracle of Meinrad and the ravens; nay, you drop the miraculous dedication of Our Lady's shrine.'

St. Meinrad was of noble race. His father, Berthold of Hohenzollern, sent him as a boy to Reichenau, an island in the Zeller See. A Benedictine abbey stood upon that isle. Of this great abbey two of Meinrad's uncles were the chiefs, and here he closed his studies, chose his part in life, and took upon himself religious vows. His youth, his learning, and his noble mien attracted every eye. A small society of monks at Bollingen, on the upper Lake of Zürich, wanting a director of their studies, begged him to accept this office. In his modesty of soul he would have put their offer by, but his superior in the convent laid the duty of acceptance on him. As he passed through Zürich to the upper Lake, he waited on the Lady abbess, who received him with the highest favour, and enriched him with an image of the Virgin and her Child, just large enough for him to carry in his arms and hang upon his convent wall. This image afterwards attained miraculous fame. From Bollingen the youthful Benedictine gazed across the lake, and peering through the lonely hills and forests on her southern borders, felt a passionate yearning rise within him to ascend those heights and seek in those dark solitudes some spot where he might hide him from the sight of living men. St. John the Baptist was his favourite saint, and, like the Nazarite, he would live alone. He crossed the lake, with nothing in his hands except his rule, his missal, and his image of the Mother and her Child. He clambered to Mount Etzel, where he dug a cave and built a cross. But shepherds from the alps and dwellers from the water-side came up to him in search of spiritual light and help; for Meinrad was a great confessor of men's sins; and though his rule was strict, and he was plain of speech, yet people flocked to him from east and west. Mount Etzel grew into a busy place, and he began to fear it, as a spot too lovely and too near the world. No hiding from the sight of men on such a hill! Behind him, in the mountains, lay a wild, impenetrable wood, then known to shepherds as the Sombre Forest. Pushing through the firs and stones he came upon a spring of water, and, the spot being rude and lonely, he was minded to accept the sign and dig his cell. He built a chapel for his image of the Virgin and her Child; he fetched his missal and his homilies from Mount Etzel; and he spent his days and years, in this wild nook, in company with two ravens, and engaged in pondering on the sacred mysteries of our faith. A crowd of people followed to his cell, where he received and helped them as of yore, until two robbers, whom he took into his cabin, thinking he was rich, laid hold of him, and clubbed him till he died.

Not finding what they sought—for Meinrad left no riches save his book, his image, and his shirt of hair—the murderers fled towards Zürich, followed by the ravens, which pursued them with avenging cries. The murderers could not drive these ravens off. At Zürich they retired into an inn; but the avenging ravens dashed against the windows of their room; got into it; and flew upon them till the magistrates of Zürich, hearing of this mystery, came up, and caused inquiry to be made. When they were brought before the court, these murderers confessed their crime.

'That miracle of the ravens is attested by your records,' says the priest; 'you have the ravens on your coat-of-arms.'

The Benedictine father smiles.

A flock of anchorites soon gathered round St. Meinrad's Cell, and lived in scattered cabins up and down the valley, till St. Eberhard built a church, in which he hung the sacred image of the Virgin and her Child. This shrine was the beginning of Einsiedeln. When the edifice was ready, Conrad, bishop of Constanz, came to consecrate it; but on going into the church at night with several of his monks to say a prayer, he was amazed to see the chapel filled with heavenly light, and Christ, attended by the four evangelists, standing at the altar, consecrating it with His own hand and voice. A cloud of angels scattered incense round; St. Michael led a choir of singers; while St. Peter and St. Gregory stood behind our Lord. The bishop lay upon the floor in prayer until eleven o'clock next day. Supposing that he was asleep, the fathers pulled his robe, on which he turned and told them all that he had seen. They thought him dreaming still. At last, consenting to proceed with the consecration, he began the rite, but hardly had he opened, when a Voice, which filled the church from crypt to roof, cried, 'Cessa, cessa, frater! Capella divinitus consecrata est!' Then Conrad paused; a greater one had done his office;

and the dedication of Our Lady's chapel was complete.

'That miracle of the consecration is attested by your records,' says the priest.

A pause. The Benedictine father seems content to let the subject drop; on noting which the priest turns round on me with a peculiar shrug.

'It was a miracle to need a good deal of attesting,' I remark.

'It is attested by St. Conrad, who composed a book—' De Secretis Secretorum '—about it, by Pope Leo VIII., by Kaiser Otto, by Ulric the monk, and many others. Leo's bull, in favour of that miracle, has been sustained by Innocent IV., Martin IV., and Nicolas IV. Ten later popes have ratified these briefs of former popes. If testimony counts for anything, that miracle of the consecration of the Virgin's chapel is a well-attested fact.'

The Benedictine father smiles, but with the faintest spectre of a smile. Again the priest looks round at me, and adds, in somewhat bantering tone: 'Like Meinrad on Mount Etzel, we have found the world too near us. If we kept it farther off, we should not send so much of Meinrad's gold to the United States.'

St. Meinrad's gold to the United States! The sneer is based on fact, and thereby hangs a tale. In 1848, alarmed by what was taking place at Fribourg and Luzern, the fathers gathered in their sheaves, and sent a goodly portion of their stock to Indiana, where they built themselves a second and what seemed a safer home. Their farm and church in the United States are managed by an English monk. As yet, the fathers have not had to fly; nor do the faithful at Einsiedeln care to talk about that property laid up in foreign lands for future use. Such worldly prudence seems to cast some doubt upon their confidence in the Virgin and her Child.

In crossing the great square again, we notice Sister Agnes at Our Lady's Spring; and help her to secure her draughts of water. At the fourteenth beck, she drops her beads, and looks a little faint.

'Have you to walk so far as the nunnery, In der Au, to sleep?'

'No, not so far. The nights are dark; the roads are very rough. We are allowed to lodge near by. To-morrow is our Festival of the Rosary. We must be up and stirring long before the daylight comes.'

CHAPTER XXII.

FEAST OF THE ROSARY.

Wha-a-ang! You start in bed. Hollo! What noise is that? What shakes the house—a strong stone house—and breaks your slumber like a shot? A gun! How can it be a gun? What maniac would be firing cannons in a church at dead of night? Some meteor must have fallen on the earth; some mountain may have slipped into the ravine. Wha-ang! Again; what can it mean? You spring upon the boards; you dash the window open; and you peer into the murky void. All gloom of mist, and patter of descending rain. A gust of wind flies at you. Puh! a flash is on your face—a crash is in your ears. A gun— assuredly a gun this time! But why this fury in the silent hours, and on the morning of a sacred day? Can these be men of Schwyz descending from the Katzenstrick once more?

You screw the window tight—observe that

it is three o'clock—and shiver into bed. You close your eyes and try to fall asleep. Five minutes—whang! ten minutes—whang! The walls vibrate, the windows fly, the doors and rafters groan. You wait the shots, and count them ;—five, seven, ten—whang, whang! At length you strike a light and ring a bell. 'What's all this row about?'

'This row,' exclaims the sleepy house-lad; 'don't you know what day it is?'

'You mean the Festival of the Rosary?'

'Yes; and that is why they fire the guns. It is Our Lady's day.'

'But why these guns?'

'Because it is Our Lady's day. Why guns? To rouse the sleepers from their beds. No man should miss the early mass on Mary's day.'

Whang!—whang! You rise and dress; for in this narrow valley, closed on every side with rocks and capped with woods, no mortal ear could close on these awakening guns. Already in the streets below you catch a sound of hurrying feet and whispering tongues. Already in the great dim square, between the village and the church, you catch the forms of spectral pilgrims, flitting through the rain and crouching at Our Lady's Spring. A light is burning in the church; and as the final gun explodes, the two tall belfries fling into the darkness such a peal of bells as men will seldom hear from convent tower except in Moscow. All the world is now astir and in the streets; men, women, children; soldiers, monks, professors; bar-maids, nurses, teachers; huddling through the darkness and the rain to early mass, in answer to that battle-cry of prayer.

At four o'clock, two hours before the sun will rise, an early mass is given before Our Lady's shrine; before the image which St. Meinrad carried to his desert cell.

This image is the subject of a hundred miracles. Three times the church has been destroyed by fire, and every time the flames have spared this piece of art. It has escaped the ancient Switzers and the modern French. A Benedictine is not fond of France; and when the French broke into Switzerland, this church and convent soon became their spoil. The Virgin's chapel was destroyed; the crowns and plaques of gold were stolen; and the sacred bones were pitched into a common sink. The image? Well;

those Frenchmen took it down; they found the robes were tinsel, and the stones were false. They carried it to Paris as a relic of the times and countries where a people, not insane, could worship stocks and stones. But when the Benedictines were restored they brought their image with them, not from France, but from the Tyrol; saying, that the statue carried off to Paris was a false one, made by cunning people, when the fathers fled, for the rapacious French to steal.

A church of ample size, arranged with choir and altar, and adorned with paint and gilding in the newest Roman style, is all a-blaze with lights and thronged with worshippers. In glow of colour and in warmth of life, the scene is Spanish and Sicilian. Above, on groin and vault, on shaft and niche, are saints and angels, arabesques and flowers, alive with red and blue, and tricked with bars and rims of gold. Below, the floors are rich with monks and nuns, with youths and girls; the men with cloaks and wallets, and the girls with red and yellow skirts. A man is kneeling here and there, but, as in Italy and Spain, the female pilgrims count as five to one. Two altars in the nave appear to draw more pilgrims than the rest—although a pilgrim needs to take these altars all in turn, lest he should vex some powerful saint. These favourites are the altars of St. Rosary and St. Meinrad, both of which are bright with paint and lamps. Above St. Rosary is painted Jacob's ladder, with the angels tripping up and down, and in a scroll these words of Scripture—'Surely the Lord is in this place.' St. Meinrad is depicted in his desert cell. Each altar has a separate crowd, and in a church so vast each crowd has room to pray apart; but when the mass commences in Our Lady's chapel, every eye is turned, and every head is bent towards this miraculous shrine.

Our Lady's chapel, dark and sombre, stands beneath the painted dome, and in the centre of a painted nave, as those who built it meant that it should look—a tomb in one vast field of flowers.

A small black shrine, with figures carved in wood and painted white, with open grill in front, and two small entrance-doors, this chapel is about the size of the Holy Sepulchre. Six lamps were once kept burning at the shrine; each Catholic Canton in the League supplying oil for one undying lamp; but now the Radicals are masters, they have let these lights die out for lack of oil. No light is wanting now; for every pilgrim has it on his soul to give one dip at least; and every corner of the shrine, from grill to shaft and ledge, is reeking with the stench, and cracking with the heat of melting wax.

A priest and his assistants stand within the holy place. Around the iron grills and sombre shafts, a mighty throng of pilgrims swarm to pray; three thousand at the least; in whom the passions that are more than mortal burn with a mysterious flame. To all these prostrate souls, the figure of the Virgin is no log of withering pine, all carved and overlaid, but an abiding eidolon, in which the woman without sin has taken up her rest. Except before the Iberian gate in Moscow, where the picture of the Black Virgin of Iberia hangs, my eyes have seen no sight like this before Our Lady's shrine. All passions seem to sway these groups by turn. One instant they are dumb with terror of the burning lights; next moment they are wild and loud with the exulting chant. Some beat their faces on the flags; some toss their arms above their heads; and some cry out in pain and passion, 'Mary, Mary! save us, save us from the deathless pit.' A dozen women start upon their feet and fumble in their skirts for coin.

'A light, give me a light!' they scream. A church official sells them dips, which they ignite and fasten to the marble shrine, till the funereal chapel is one mass of burning stars. A low and musical voice intones the mass. A tiny silver bell rings out the points; and when the host is raised, a gunshot crashes through the aisles, and every heart leaps up. A pause—a listening wonder—till the echoes die away from choir and vault; and then a cry of rapture greets that miracle which is renewed from day to day—that transformation of the actual flesh and blood into the visible bread and wine.

When mass is ended, every face seems flushed with an unearthly light, as though these pilgrims have been blessed with glimpses of an unknown world. It passes from them in a moment like a smile; but while it lingers on their brows and in their eyes, these shepherds from the alps, these weavers from the hamlets, are as lovely in their rapture of expression as a brotherhood of painted saints.

From five to six we loiter in the ample nave; inspect the votive offerings nailed on door and slung on rail—a waxen doll, a bit of half-burnt rag, a daub of some miraculous cure—each offering with an image of the Virgin and her Child; move forward with the crowd from shrine to shrine, and drop a prayer at each in turn—St. Anne, St. Joseph, and St. Benedict in chief; peruse the list of abbots who have reigned and died here, from St. Eberhard, Count of Franconia, 959, down to the Reverend Celestin Müller, of Schmerikon, Canton St. Gallen, 1845; including—third upon the list—St. Gregory, (called a son of Edward the Elder, king of England, brother-in-law of kaiser Otto), in whose person the abbot of Einsiedeln was created an imperial prince.

At six o'clock the sun rises, and at six o'clock there is a special service for the rising of our convent sun, St. Meinrad. In this special service we include St. Eberhard, and the other holy men who aided him to found this temple in a desert place. When this is done, a priest and acolyte repair to one of the side altars, where they chant a verse, and then turn round upon the kneeling crowds, and bless the rosaries which the pilgrims carry in their hands. Some pilgrims take advantage of the priest to get his blessing on a dozen things besides their beads—a charm, a crucifix, a bunch of ribbons, nay, a box of toys—by holding them in front of him together with the beads. No charge is made for blessing these mementoes of Einsiedeln, but a pilgrim who has money in his purse is taught the duty of investing some of it with God. Upstairs there is a passage with a grill, at which a priest is stationed to receive such gifts, and bless the bringers with a special grace.

At seven o'clock, the abbot, Heinrich IV., comes down into the church, attended by his clergy, and ascends his throne, while three superior priests perform high mass in the grand sanctuary; a picturesque and noble rite, regarded merely as a work of musical and scenic art. Three organs and a band assist the choir; these organs, raised aloft in singing galleries, are extremely fine in tone. A learned Benedictine, Pater Schubiger, known as author of the 'Roses de Marie,' makes the music, and in part conducts the service. Abbot Heinrich Schmid, of Baar, in Canton Zug, a grave and passive man, with ample face, white hair, and noble aspect, looks the prince which pious pilgrims call him, though his temporal rank and power are gone. The three officiating priests are richly clothed; the singers are concealed from sight; and when the host is raised—the cannon fired—three thousand kneeling figures bend their temples to the floor, and fling their arms about in ecstasies of pain and bliss.

At eight o'clock there is a sermon, chiefly an account, in ghostly phrase, of the fifteen mysteries of the rosary. A rosary was a form of prayer before it was a string of beads—a form of prayer divided into three parts and fifteen decades—so called from each decade retaining ten Ave Marias. To say a whole rosary, with its fifteen Pater Nosters, and its ten times fifteen Ave Marias, is to do a good and perfect work. It is a saving office of the Church; a solace to the poor, the ignorant, the despised of men; to those for whom our Lord was sent, from whom He chose his twelve Apostles, and on whom He built his everlasting Church.

At nine we break our fast; but soon return from inn and guest-room to the confessional. This confessional, called a Penitentiary, and dedicated to the Sinner of Magdala, is a low and vaulted chapel, built among the graves of ancient monks—a dark and noisome place, in which a single lamp burns dimly, and a watery kind of light creeps in through grated openings in the wall. A dirge is being howled behind a screen. A solitary priest is serving in the gloom. Dark frescoes, chiefly smoke and fire, adorn the roof. Along this chapel of the Magdalen, two rows of penitential chairs are placed for the confessors and the pilgrims—twenty-eight in number—each confessional marked, according to the language spoken by the ghostly father, as either German, French, or Romonsch. In each a priest is seated, listening to a tale of sin and shame, while troops of penitents are kneeling, rank on rank, each waiting for his call. At some confessionals two penitents are busy with one priest. Much practice makes men perfect in all trades, even that of searching hearts. These fathers have no time to lose. They shrive four hundred sinners on an average every day the whole year round. To-day the number to be heard is close upon two thousand souls; and, let these fathers labour as they may, this crowd of sinners yearning to be cleansed will not be all confessed and shriven before the hour of midnight chimes.

At three o'clock come vespers in the sanctuary, sung by an invisible choir. At the cry of praise all voices drop, and every one kneels down. First ring the boyish altos, then the men roll in with middle note and bass. All female lips are closed, for in these Catholic offices a woman has no place. At half-past three o'clock the fathers march in ranks along the nave, into the Virgin's chapel, where they chant a special service at her shrine, A pilgrim looks upon this office as the crowning worship of his day. His heart may now be light and glad; he may have told his sin and got his shrift. His beads and trinkets have been blessed, and in his rapture he is like a little child. Instead of praying, he can praise; instead of grovelling, he can now adore. When this great act is over, there is still more blessing of the rosaries, along with books and medals, candles, rings, and rolls of wax.

At four o'clock we go away to dine, and come again at seven o'clock for complines. It is dark again; and yet the duties of the Penitentiary are still going on. A gun-shot breaks the murmur of a thousand eager tongues. Lay brothers sweep the lights out; and a crowd of pilgrims turn their faces to the world. Yet many stay behind; and when you steal into the church at midnight you may find some penitents lingering in the Magdalen's vault.

CHAPTER XXIII.

LAST OF THE BENEDICTINES.

'YES : we are the last,' says Pater Morel, Rector of the seminary, as we cross the square; 'the last òf our old Order in this country, where we held in former days so many abbeys of the highest class—St. Gallen, Muri, Rheinau, Dissentis, and Pfäffers, for example. All these great establishments have fallen. We, of Meinrad's Cell, are left alone; it may be, under Providence, for our labour's sake. Who else would take the charge of all these penitents?'

With the sole exception of Einsiedeln, all the Benedictine abbeys in this country have been seized by orders from the Cantonal officers, and their lands and goods divided by the state, as convents have been seized by orders from the royal officers in Italy and Spain. These abbeys only suffer in the common wreck of all religious houses, whether those of Capuchins, Augustines,

Jesuits, or Franciscans. The Switzers want their money, and these Switzers take this money with no more remorse of mind than the Italians feel in seizing Rome.

One instance may be cited. On a spot of land surrounded by the Rhine, and looking over into Baden, stands the great Benedictine abbey of Rheinau; once a famous seat of learning and a home of all the liberal arts. A school is wanted by the public, and as Rheinau is supposed to be extremely rich, a bill is brought into the Council, authorising the state to close that abbey, turn the monks adrift, and seize their lands and goods for public use. In vain the fathers plead that what they have belongs to Holy Church. In vain they offer to divide their wealth. In vain they ask for leave to found a college, build an hospice, raise the pay of Catholic priests. The bill is passed, the abbey seized. A sum of 3,328,000 francs is taken from the Order, and dispersed as follows:—

To the parish of Rheinau	250,000 frs.
Pensions to dispossessed fathers	300,000
Given to Catholic Communes	700,000
Spent on schools	2,078,000
	3,328,000

What is done at Rheinau has been done elsewhere, according to the local need. The great abbey of St. Gallen has been turned into a barrack and infirmary; that of Dissentis, from which the Prince-abbot, Christian von Castelberg, defied and damned the Swiss Reformers, has been turned into a secondary school for boys. The not less splendid abbey of Pfäffers is a lunatic asylum, and the abbot's palace at Ragatz an inn.

Five reasons have been given by writers on the Benedictine Order for the favour which surrounds the fathers at Einsiedeln:—first, the high protection of their Virgin; next, the grace of their religious calling; third, the homeliness of their manners; then, the state of their relations with great people; fifth, the visible utility of their presence on the spot.

There is another reason still—the policy of that homely saw which hints that a wise housekeeper should not kill a bird that lays him golden eggs.

The porches of the abbey look into the town; a very curious town; what Canterbury was when knight and reeve, and clerk and nun, rode into it on pilgrimage with the abbot and the wife of Bath. Einsiedeln is a town of inns and shops, and all ablaze with signs and flags. St. Meinrad has a separate flag from Canton Schwyz,—a blood-red field, on which, instead of a simple cross, is limned the Virgin and her Child. St. Meinrad's banner floats from nearly every door and cill. One line of tall, squat houses fronts the church and belfries; every house in that long line, save one, a public inn. These inns are known by saintly names—St. John, St. Joseph, and St. Catharine; Holy Anchorites, Three Kings and Cloister Gardens — with the Sun, the Forest, and the Peacock. Pilgrims of the wiser sort avoid all inns with saintly names. In rear of these large houses stand a motley group of taverns, dropping in the scale of comfort as they back to narrow lanes and courts, until you find some poorer guest-rooms, where the peasant-pilgrims lodge by tens and twenties in a single room. In such poor rooms the pilgrims pack themselves by night on shelves. The charge is nowhere high; and in these modest stalls it is one penny each, paid down at night before ascending to your shelf.

Much trade is driven in relics, pictures, beads, and photographs—in crosses, medals, rings, and cotton prints — in earrings, candles, books — in amulets, gingerbread, and charms—as well as in the things that will not keep—in sausages, cigars, and schnaps. The street is full of shops, and the arcades beside Our Lady's spring are full of shops. Yet this large Gentile court is not enough, and wings of timber-sheds run off on either side the convent walls, like booths in country fairs, where objects still more trashy — tinsel saints and wooden dolls—are spread along the boards for sale.

The dealers in these articles of devotion have a bad name in the convent, which these dealers seem to treat as lawful prize, provided for them by their saints. In fact, the Commune of Einsiedeln claim the abbey of Einsiedeln as their own. They, not the fathers, are, they say, the permanent owners. They are natives of the soil, while many of the fathers are not Switzers born. The fathers come and go; the villagers live and die upon the spot.

Some years ago, when putting in this claim, the Commune seized the lordship of this abbey, with a great part of the forests, lands, and farms belonging to its lord. An armed band profaned the holy place, and Heinrich Schmid, the abbot, was obliged to yield. The last poor remnant of his princely power was gone; and henceforth, he and his must keep on terms with village mayor and village council if they wish to live in peace. Where once the abbots reigned, they have to sue; and men who used to grovel in the dust before their thrones, now take their money and their goods as lightly as a German company levies war-tax on the conquered French. The Commune feel, however, that they must not go too far; it would not serve their turn to drive these fathers from St. Meinrad's Cell into some other place. They might secrete their Virgin once again, and then the tide of pilgrims would be turned another way.

In seeking strength abroad against these foes at home, the fathers are supposed to turn with too much longing to each rising sun. When kaiser Francis Joseph was a mighty potentate, the monks approached him with a prayer that he would take them under his august protection, like his ancestors the Dukes of Austria. Francis Joseph sent them gracious words, together with his portrait. After Solferino, they approached Napoleon III. Hortense, on making pilgrimage to Einsiedeln, wrote these words: 'I wish to place myself and my infants under the protection of the Holy Virgin.' They reminded him of these good words; he sent his portrait, and a gilded chandelier. They next approached the Pope, and got his portrait and his blessing. Prussia could not be neglected, Lutheran though she is; and they contrived to get a small and unobtrusive portrait of her king. But after Sadowa, they felt how much that small and unobtrusive portrait was unworthy of so great a man. Reminding Wilhelm that St. Meinrad was a Hohenzollern, they succeeded in procuring for their abbey an enlarged and powerful portrait of the kaiser-king.

Except the pilgrim's mite, the fathers have no visible income to maintain their sacred edifice and conventual buildings other than the proceeds of their schools. These Benedictine schools, of which my host is Rector, have a fame in Catholic homes, like that of Zürich schools in scientific homes. The Reverend Pater Morel is a poet, of the class and rank of our own Southwell. His religious reveries, mostly turning on the graces and perfections of his Patroness, are read in many cities of the Old World and the New. A copy of his poems lies before me in two volumes, with the imprint of New York. But, like his brethren of a brighter time, he is a man of many sides; a critic, an historical writer, and an antiquary. In his hands the seminaries seem to hold their own; two hundred names are on his books; and yet, in going through the class-rooms, one is struck with the great number of foreign scholars in these famous schools. Not many of the traders of Einsiedeln send their children to the monks.

A goodly number of these pupils are intended for the priesthood; but the sciences and arts are widely taught. Much time is given to music in its many branches; singing, both in solo and in chorus; playing on the several kinds of horn, presiding at the organ, and composing masses, overtures, and psalms. A thousand years ago, the Benedictines of these districts had a great renown as singers. Pater Schubiger, ex-chapel-master of Einsiedeln, has composed a history of the St. Gallen school of singing from the eighth century to the twelfth. A something of this antique fame remains, and since the Benedictine abbey of St. Gallen was suppressed, this art, like many of her sisters—painting, carving, casting, building,—has to seek a home in this last refuge of the learned and despairing monks.

A hundred members make the last society of this illustrious order; seventy fathers, fifteen acolytes, and fifteen lay brethren; in the whole a hundred souls devoted to religious work; including all that books and arts can offer to their church. These numbers may not be increased, though the conventual buildings might contain five hundred more. One hundred fathers are supposed to be enough to do what needs be done; to say the masses, hear confessions, sing vespers, and receive the pilgrim pence. Schwyz rules it so; and from the Canton there is no appeal.

All other bodies in this country have some liberty of action. Take the League of Grütli, the Firing Club, the International, the Society of Public Usefulness; all these societies, and hundreds like them, are allowed to make their own rules, admit their own members, and increase their numbers as they please. The Benedictine fathers at Einsiedeln, though they owned this hamlet long before the name of Schwyz arose, are not permitted by their Canton to receive one monk beyond the hundred fixed for them by law.

A hundred fathers are not many for the work they have to do. Much farming, gardening, cooking, carving, painting, modelling, and the like, must needs be done. Not only have the great basilica and the convent to be kept in order, but a number of dependent shrines demand some care. St. Meinrad's well, a chapel on the road to Biberbruck, requires some care; the chapel on Mount Etzel needs some care; the nunnery In der Au requires some care. Fifteen lay monks are not too many for these various tasks. Nor are these brethren men to waste their time in hedge and ditch. Brother Mannhardt is an excellent carver. He has carved and built an altar-piece, which, in a showy Roman style, is not unworthy of his convent in her better days. Brother Blätter, a professor of design, not only teaches in his class-room, but repairs and ornaments his church. One learned brother has the care of coins and medals, while another takes the stables and the farms.

A dozen services a-day, not counting the confessions, have to be performed in public, with the pomp and awe of Catholic worship. Schools have to be kept, and visits paid. Some study must be done, and many visitors, who take up time, must be received. A band of seventy monks and fifteen acolytes would not seem many for these various labours; but the service of confession is the greatest work of all. If seventy monks had nothing else to do but shrive the penitents, they could not lead an idle life. Above four hundred pilgrims kneel to them each day throughout the year; six sinners to each monk the whole year round.

Yet some of these hard-working fathers find the time to write; and write such books as learned men can praise. The abbot, Heinrich, has the reputation of a scholar. Pater Brandis has an European name.

'We are the last,' sighs Pater Morel, as we pass from room to room—now echoing to our steps—of this magnificent seat of learning. 'Yes; St. Gallen, Muri, Dissentis, were once our rivals in the work of God; but they are gone the way of instruments used up and thrown aside; and we of Meinrad's Cell are left to carry on the work alone. We do our best, although it is not much. We try to keep alive some sense of sacred art— some love of sacred music—some desire for sacred letters—in an age devoted to material things. We do our duty, as the task is laid upon us, and we hope to do that duty to the end.'

CHAPTER XXIV.

CONFLICT OF THE CHURCHES.

No cause could justify the wrongs—the open and intentional wrongs — inflicted on religious orders in this country, but a strong conviction working in men's minds, and driving them to acts beyond excuse on lower grounds, that these religious orders are the foreposts of an enemy planted on their soil. In such a case appeals are vain; the public safety is the highest law.

No man with eyes to see can live in Switzerland a month without perceiving that this strong conviction, whether it be right or wrong, is one of the primary forces in all public life. What else has driven the Jesuits from the soil? Their case is very hard. A man is born in Bern; he goes to school in Paris; he returns in after-life to Bern, with five or six of his old school-fellows. He and they are members of some foreign league or order. No one cares about them. Every Switzer is a member of some dozen leagues, societies, and orders—native orders, foreign orders, private, civic, and religious orders. He begins by being a member of his Commune, of his Canton, of his League. He is a member of the Sunday Society, the Society of Public Usefulness, the Swiss Alpine Club, the Band of Pio Nono, the Grütli Society, the International, the Society of St. Vincent de Paul, the League of Peace and Liberty, the Federal Shooting Association, the Society of Freemasons. He may be a member also of many local guilds and orders; singing circles, democratic clubs, academies of art, gymnastic unions, fire brigades, trade societies, antiquarian and historical societies, and natural-history clubs. A Switzer has organization on the brain. In two Swiss Cantons, and one Half-canton, an inquiry made into the number of societies known, and registered, gives the following facts:—

In Schaffhausen,	87 Societies to	.	35,500 souls.
,, Baselstadt,	126 ,,	,, .	40,683
,, Geneva,	220 ,,	,, .	82,876

In the several Cantons more than four thousand orders, bands, and societies are known. These bands and orders are of every sort and size, with ends the most dissimilar in view. In Switzerland a man may be a Turk, a Jew, a Buddhist, a Confucian. No matter; if he is a Switzer born he has his natural right; and if he be a stranger in the land, he is protected by the Federal law.

But if the little band should call themselves Jesuits, down the Canton comes with heavy hand upon them. In Geneva, Jews have built a synagogue; and no one could object if Parsees were to build a temple, and Mohammedans a mosque. But neither in Geneva, nor in any Canton of the League, dare any one erect a Jesuit college. If a Switzer joins the Mormons, no one interferes with him; but if he joins the Company of Jesus he foregoes his national rights.

To pass and to preserve a law which stands in open contradiction to all other laws, there must be stern conviction in the popular mind that Jesuitism and freedom cannot grow together in a common soil.

'It is a conflict of the world against the church,' the Jesuits cry, on one side in the fray. 'It is a victory of the native church against a foreign priest,' reply the Radicals on the other side. The Jesuits urge that every shred the world has ever saved from wreck is now at stake; that learning, order, art, and freedom are about to perish; and that nothing can redeem mankind but full and prompt submission to the Holy See. 'You have your choice,' shouts General Castella, in a recent speech to an excited crowd at Bulle, 'of two things one—holy water or petroleum!'

The liberals answer that the world is pushing on, that men are better lodged and fed, that boys and girls are better taught, that public liberties are more secure, with every passing year. They say this progress is the working out of providential laws. A liberal puts an Evangelical district in the scale against a Catholic district—such as that of Appenzell-outer-Rhoden against Appenzell-inner-Rhoden—and demands a verdict on the evidence of eye and ear.

In outer aspect these Half-cantons have the differences of Canton Bern and Canton Valais. In the lower country, though the village may be built of frames, the style is pretty, the arrangement neat. A fountain and a running water occupy the centre. Near it stand the village church, the council-chamber, and the primary school. Each cottage has a garden to itself. A creeper climbs up every stair, and hangs from almost every roof. The click and whirr of looms are heard from every open window, and the little folk go singing on their way to school. The streets are clean, the markets well supplied, and every one you meet is warmly clad. But in the upper country things look poor and bare. Few villagers are seen. The people dwell in scattered huts, with styes and stables on the ground, and sleeping-rooms above them, like the folks in Biscay and Navarre. These huts, though strongly knit, are rudely planned and roughly built. Each herdsman lives apart from all his fellows, whom he only meets at mass, at wrestling-match, and public-house. The lads can read and write, for they are Switzers, subject to the Cantonal law; but books and journals are unknown among them, saving here and there some lives of saints and popular sheets, containing scraps of old-wives' lore in place of general and exciting news.

The Protestant Half-canton grows in wealth and numbers, while the Catholic Half-canton lingers on in poverty and weakness; for the first takes in all strangers, irrespective of their creed, gives ready welcome to ideas on all subjects, and adopts without delay improvements in the loom—her chief domestic engine; while the second shuts her gates on all the world—on Protestants of every country, and on Catholics who are not natives of the Canton—keeps her antique sports and dress, retains her shepherd industries as they existed in the middle ages, keeps her feast-days and her wrestling-matches, feeds on coarse rye-bread and acid curds, and holds in proud contempt the arts by which her neighbours thrive.

All Cantons of Teutonic race, in which the Catholics are in bulk the people, such as Uri, Zug, Luzern, and Unterwalden, are in most things very much like Catholic Appenzell. All Cantons of Teutonic race, in which the Protestants are in bulk the people, such as Basel, Bern, Schaffhausen, Glarus, and Thurgau, are in most things very much like Evangelical Appenzell.

In Catholic Cantons there is one exception to this rule of dirt and dearth—the city of Luzern. This city has a bright and cheery aspect, more like Zürich and Lausanne than Altdorf, Stanz, and Zug. This cheery face is not a product of the system and the soil. It is a new and foreign growth. Not long ago, Luzern, the home of priestly rule, the shrine of mercenary troops, was little better than a fever-bed. The dykes were weak, the waters swelled into the streets, and every flood left pestilence behind. But strangers come into the town, attracted by her beauty, who enrich it with their gold. For them, wide streets are cleared, stone bridges built, fine walks laid out. A line of great hotels extends along the lake. But enterprise without implies some enterprise within. A man who takes much pains to set his house in order soon begins to set his mind in order likewise. Even in Luzern a democratic party has grown up, who hold their own against the priests.

This conflict of the democrats and theocrats is not confined to the Germanic Cantons. It is equally appparent in the French. In Carteret's report on the Project of Law for Canton Geneva, it came out in stronger terms than any used in Zürich, Bern, and Basel. Every liberal would be glad to stop all public payments for the Calvinistic chair of theology in Geneva; but while sums are voted in the Catholic Cantons for the teaching of a Roman catechism in the primary schools, the liberals of Geneva hold their hands, and keep the chair provided by the Protestant constitution of their city. What is right for one side in the strife is right for all. The principle is one thing, and the practice is another. 'The instruction given by the religious corporations,' says M. Carteret, with a glance at Catholic teaching, 'is not teaching of a kind to form republican citizens worthy of this noble name. These congregations, in a land like ours, where the country makes such efforts to bring a good education to every man's door, can only fill a gap. There ought to be no gap. Their object is to train the young impressionable minds confided to their care into a firm belief that civil life should be subordinated to the church. When that idea gains the upper hand, alas for the people! One direct and certain means of meeting this great obstacle exists: deprive the religious corporations altogether of their right to teach!' But Carteret refrains from carrying out his own suggestion; seeing that he can only do so in his own Calvinistic Canton, while the Catholic Cantons will not follow in his wake. He therefore leaves the chair of Protestant theology untouched.

No plan for reconciling these two parties in the Canton can be found. The points of difference lie in the essentials, not in the externals; and the systems are at war beyond the power of gods and men to cool their rage. Democracy will not give way; theocracy will not give way. 'All men are equal,' runs the liberal creed, which takes no notice of original sin, the fall of man, and the prerogatives of a priestly class. 'Men have no rights,' says Rome, which holds her power from heaven, and scoffs at rights of man; for men are fallen creatures, lost to grace, and only to be saved by strict obedience to her law. One creed is lay and civil, while the other creed assumes to be divine. The genius and the method are alike opposed. While Bern and Zürich lean on Luther and the great reformers, Zug and Altdorf lean on Loyola and the great inquisitors. One system would excite, expand, and quicken thought; the other would subdue, contract, and paralyse it. Zürich frames a code by which it hopes to make the boy a pious, reasoning, independent man; while Zug and Uri frame their codes to make the boy a docile, listening, and submissive man.

Each side has much to say in favour of its rule.

'Born in a free state,' the liberals say; 'we have to teach our children how to live, and how to keep their freedom. We avoid contention in the schools. We wish our sons to be religious; but we will not have them quarrelling over creeds. We recognise a Christian life beyond the class-room. Of this Christian life, the love of God, the fellowship of man, the purity of morals, are the noblest parts.'

'All that is only negative,' the Jesuits answer. 'Your pretence of freedom is a dream. All souls are lost; and your devices will not save one soul from hell. We dare not trifle with our task. We are appointed to our work by God, and not by man. We cannot ask your councillors, elected by the lost ones, how we are to do our duty. When the blind conduct the blind, they fall into a pit; and lo, the pit you march towards is the pit of fire!'

This conflict of the churches rages in the schools.

CHAPTER XXV.

SCHOOL.

IN Switzerland, the primary business of the state is keeping school.

A School is one of the first things present to the eyes of a Swiss child, and one of the last things present to the mind of a Swiss man. It comes to him in his cradle and attends him to his grave. He could not cast it from him if he would; he would not cast it from him if he could.

A Swiss child dreams of school as urchins in an English city dream of work. He knows it is his fate in life. He sees his brother and his sister go to school; he sees them bring their lessons home; he sees them rise at dawn to learn their tasks. If he is stout of limb and clear of sight, his turn will come, and he must also troop to school. On coming to a certain age— in some, the age of six, in some of seven—his right to stay at home, to play at top and make mud-pies, will cease. He is a member of his Commune, and the Commune will not suffer him to live and die a pig. The school will seize him, hold him fast for years, and rear him into what he is to be: a banker, goatherd, student, tinker, what not; but in any case it will not lose its grasp until he grows into a man. But then an infant Swiss dreams pleasantly of school, while urchins in our country dream unpleasantly of work. If school is fate to a Swiss child, the vision comes to him in likeness of a fairy, not a hag.

Among the many quaint old fountains in these streets of Bern—with heroes, knights, and ladies on the shafts—there is a fountain in the cornmarket, with an ogre, known to Bernese little folks as kindli-fresser — children-catcher,—looking up the street. This ogre has a tooth for boys and girls, and clutches them as they go by. A child is disappearing down the monster's throat; three children flutter in the monster's wallet; and a bunch of children twist and wriggle in the monster's belt. That monster will devour them one and all. Grown men dispute about the legend of this ogre in the streets of Bern. One holds him out to be a feudal lord, another as an emblem of the church. A pastor tells me that the ogre who devours his offspring is the Revolution; and a sharp young student from the neighbouring college whispers he is only Time. But neither man nor boy in Bern imagines that this ogre represents the School. A noble lady, sweet of face and firm of purpose, with her arms about the children's necks, would be to man and boy alike the type of School.

The fairest edifice a Swiss can see when he goes out to walk is his village school, his city school, his Cantonal school, according as he happens to reside in country or in town. A jail, a workhouse, nay, a town-hall, may nestle in some corner where a curious eye might miss it; but school, a college, an academy, is sure to be in sight, the pride of every village slope and every city square. In Zürich and Lausanne, the intellectual capitals of Switzerland — Teutonic capital and Latin capital—the noblest buildings are the public schools. If we except the Federal Hall at Bern, the Polytechnic in Zürich is the finest edifice in this country; fine alike in site, proportion, fitness, and display. 'Our children,' says to me a sage professor, 'are so much accustomed to regard the school-house as the foremost building in a city, that they fall into the drollest errors when they go abroad.' He tells me, as an illustration of such errors, that some years ago he took his daughter, then a child of ten, to France, and, being at Versailles, he heard her clap her hands, and cry with glee, 'Look here, papa; here is the school-house! Look!' It was the garden front of that huge pile.

It is the same,—or very near the same,—when you are out of town. You walk into some deep and sombre gorge, with jagged heights and foaming torrents, where the pines can hardly cling, a châlet here and there, high up, on what appears an inaccessible ledge of rock, and near you not a sound, except the crash of falling trees just breaking the oppressive monotone of rushing floods. 'No school in such a gorge,' you haply say, when, lo! a square, white building rises in your front. In England such a thing would be a shooting-box, and here it is a village school. In less secluded nooks these buildings are on larger scale. Take that of Sarnen. Smiling on the bright, green water, stands the finest edifice in the Canton, and of course it is a public school. Wander round

St. Gallen; that St. Gallen which was once a seat of Benedictine learning, and is now the seat of a new trade in lace. One side of the fine public park is occupied by the Cantonal school,—a noble edifice even in this land of noble schools. Even at Einsiedeln, the great basilica is fronted by a handsome Communal school.

The larger number of these schools belong to the Communes; for in every hamlet where there may be twenty boys and girls, the mayor and council must provide a school and hire a master. Next to the Communal schools in number stand the burgher schools, which are supported by the towns; and after these the Cantonal schools, which are supported by the state. The Canton is the state. As yet there is but one Federal school in Switzerland, the Polytechnic in Zürich, which has now become for all the world a model school of practical life. A great desire is felt in Zürich, Bern, Geneva, and Lausanne, to found a Federal university of the highest class—to challenge Bonn and Heidelberg, if not Berlin. The Federal constitution gives the power to found it; but, as yet the project has been chilled by local jealousies, the fruit of those diversities of race, of creed, of speech, which make us wonder that a Switzerland exists at all. But several of the Cantons have their universities on a smaller scale, and with their faculties more or less complete. Basel has a university. Bern has a university. Zürich, Neufchatel, Geneva, have their own universities. Vaud, Luzern, St. Gallen, and Ticino, each of these Cantons has a separate university. No people in the world can boast of so many seats of learning in proportion to their number as the Switzers can.

The festivals and holidays of a Switzer are connected with his life at school. Each change is made the pretext for a feast. On going to school there is a feast; on leaving school there is a feast; at every stage of his advance there is a feast. There is vacation feast, assembling feast; when a new teacher comes there is a feast, and when a teacher leaves there is a feast. The school is made to him by public and by private acts a centre of all happy thoughts and times. It shares the joys of home and the rewards of church. At school a Swiss boy finds his mates with whom he learns to sing and play, to drill and shoot. The teacher is to him a father. With this teacher he will grow into a man, assisted on his way with care and love, unmixed with either foolish fondness or paternal pride. With him, and with his mates, the lad will take his country strolls, collecting rocks and plants; will push his boat across the lake, and dive into the secrets of the ancient water-folk; will pass by train into some neighbouring Commune where the arts are other than he sees at home. All bright and pleasant things are grouped about him; and in after-time, when farm and counter occupy his cares, these class-room days will seem to him the merriest of his life.

The school, the pupil, and the teacher, are for ever in the public eye. The scholars promenade the streets with music, flags, and songs. All men make room for them—salute them—glory in them, as the highest product of their state.

CHAPTER XXVI.

DEMOCRACY AT SCHOOL.

ATTENTION to his school is not a fixed and formal business to a Switzer, as it might be to a Briton and a Frank, but an unceasing and engrossing duty from his cradle to his grave. The school is with a Switzer always—as a child and as a man. No sooner has he ceased to be a pupil, than he starts into a principal. The village schools are governed by the villagers, and as a member of his village, be he preacher, woodman, goat-herd, inn-keeper, he must take his share in managing these public schools. He has to build them, to conduct them, and to keep them up. He has to choose the teacher and director, and to pay a portion of their stipends from his private purse. In time he is a parent with his little ones to tend and train. Then opens up a new relation to his village schools. He is a visitor, on private even more than public grounds. Each parent has a right to visit and inspect the school, to see the teacher, and consult the records of his child. Good teachers welcome these parental visits; for a parley with the father helps a teacher with his child. The circle of his duty is complete, and so a Switzer never can forget his school, and what concerns his school.

School politics are public politics. With the church and chapel make the popular politics; but in a Switzer's mind, there is an earlier stage of thought than either church or chapel reaches, and that earlier stage is only to be got at in the school.

In many Cantons there is some assertion in the fundamental law that the true end of public instruction is to combine democracy with religion, that every boy attending at a public school may grow up into a good citizen and a good Christian. In the law of Zürich it is said, 'The People's schools shall train the children of all classes, on a plan agreed upon, to be intelligent men, useful citizens, and moral and religious beings.' In the law of Luzern it is laid down that 'The school affords to every boy and girl capable of education the means of developing their mental and physical faculties, of training them for life in the family, in the community, in the church, and in the state, of putting them in the way to gain their future bread.' In Vaud the law declares that 'Teaching in the public schools shall be in accordance with the principles of Christianity and democracy.' In the law of Thurgau it is stated that 'The general aim of a primary school shall be to call out the power and talents of the children, so as to give them the knowledge and capacity of citizen-life, and to train them to be moral and religious men and women.' Almost every Canton puts a clear announcement of this principle in front—the business of a public teacher is to make his boys good Republicans and good Christians.

But the rule thus stated in the form of law is subject to revision year by year. The Jesuits and their party put religion first; and if they had their way would make it first and last. The liberals bring democracy to the front; and some among them, if they had their way, would make it all in all. With us, elections mostly turn on trade, alliances, and policy; in Switzerland, they mostly turn on school affairs; and hence the fundamental laws are in a stage of ebb and flow, as the conservative party and the democratic party gain the upper hand.

In Zürich there was recently a question in debate which set the city in a blaze. A new girls' school was wanted; every one allowed it, though a stranger might have fancied there were schools enough. The only question was, in which locality the citizens should build that school. Two parties came into the front—a clerical party and a liberal party; those who put religion first, and those who put democracy first. 'Let us build this school for females near the minster,' said the clerical party, 'for the female mind is more susceptible than the male; and if we keep the women, we shall always have the men.' The radical party met them with a counter-cry: 'No more connexion of the church and school; the clergy have no business in the class-room: let us build on neutral ground—beyond the ancient walls, among the vineyards, in the sunshine.' Public policy was with the radicals. No ground was vacant near the minster save the public square, and open places are so rare in Zürich that a project for invading one of them with stone and mortar meets with public opposition like a project with ourselves

s

for trenching on a public park. The war of words grew hot; elections turned upon it; till the clerical party got the sober people, known as *pères de famille*, on their side. These fathers said their girls should grow beneath the shadow of the minster; it was better for them; it was more respectable; it was their fate. And so the school was built on the ancient cloisters, round the graves of venerable monks. A slice of public ground was added from the public square.

In Bern a new girls' school is wanted. The site must be a fine one; yea, the very best in Bern. But sites are difficult to find in this old city, where the narrow ridge of ground is occupied from gate to bridge with ancient houses. There are left the public gardens, called the Lesser Ramparts, where the bands perform, the citizens walk, the children play, and strangers watch the sun set on the Bernese alps. Can any part of this delicious garden be surrendered? Yes; for one great purpose, and that purpose only—for a school. The site is given; but when the plans are drawn, it is discovered that some lime-trees of enormous size and matchless beauty—

trees which scent the air and cool the paths —must be destroyed. A second public pang— and they are gone. No pride and glory of the town must stand between a Switzer and his school.

In Lausanne you find the natives talking much, and wisely, of an inter-cantonal movement in support of what is held in certain towns to be 'the just influence' of the French-speaking section of the League. That section is much weaker than the German-speaking section; but in days gone by it held a share of power beyond the value of its numbers on account of its superior learning, energy, and dash. But now the tables have been turned, for German science has beaten French science, just as German arms have subdued French arms. Lausanne is not the literary capital; that supremacy has gone to Zürich. Geneva is no longer the political centre; that supremacy has gone to Bern. Fact and fear have roused the Gallic Cantons into crusade for the preservation of their rights. Professor Eugène Rambert, of Lausanne, first sounded the alarm. Professor Rambert lives in Zürich, where he holds the Chair of Literature. Aware of what is going on, he sees that 'La Suisse Romande' is losing ground, 'La Suisse Germanique' gaining ground. He calls his countrymen to arms. A party meet in the Hôtel de Ville, Lausanne — the men of Neufchatel, Geneva, Vaud, and Valais — when the state of things is carefully explained, and a proposal made to found a League of French-speaking Cantons to defend themselves against the ever-increasing German force. But how are they to hold their own? By artifice, corruption, violence? Not a dream of such things clouds their minds. The meeting sees and says it is a question of the public schools. French education is below the mark — it ought to be improved; and the Société Intercantonale proposes to revise and widen the superior education in the three French-speaking cities of Lausanne, Geneva, and Neufchatel. But how? By means, says Rambert, of a French University in Celtic Switzerland. Professor Rambert is a native of Lausanne, and he proposes to erect this Federal University in Lausanne. But here creeps in once more the sign of race. Instead of urging that the three French-speaking cities should subscribe the money and begin the work, these Celtic

Switzers ask their common country—in the main Teutonic — to provide the means. The League, they say, is rich; the Canton poor. The Communes are already taxed beyond their strength; the Cantons cannot bear fresh burthens; let a generous country pay!

CHAPTER XXVII.

GENEVA.

A BAND, a line of flags; much patter of small feet, with now and then a swell of fervid song; some fifteen hundred girls in white; a troop of magistrates and councillors, pastors, teachers, foreign consuls; then a second band, with firemen in their casques, and landwehr in their uniforms; some fifteen hundred boys in line of march; soft babble of young voices, in the intervals of drums and trumpets.

Scene—the English Garden at Geneva. Time —the afternoon of Tuesday, June the twenty-seventh. Group—the pupils of the primary schools. Occasion—the completion of the half-year's school-work. Prizes have been given to the deserving scholars. Lists of those most worthy of such honours have been read aloud. The magistrates of the republic have addressed them all in cheery and exciting words. It is a great day in their lives. They are the heroes of one happy hour; and all their faces glow with inner fire. A word is given—the bugles sound—the lines begin to move; and soon the English Garden is behind us. For the last three days the skies have opened all their gates; this morning brought a pause in the great roar of rain; and as the heads of columns quit the ground a gleam of sunshine shoots to right and left, and soon the city and the lake are bathed in golden light. The Canton is agog with joy. All men make way for the procession. ' Ha! the merry ones! Good children! Soldiers of the Lord!' are some of many greetings, as the boys and girls troop forward, pass the quays, and winding by the Molard, up the Rue Corraterie, reach the Electoral Palace, where the magistrates receive them, and regale them. After honest fare and kindly speech, the children march to the theatre, where conjurors and showmen entertain them; then to the Plainpalais, where all the city goes to meet them; and a happy day is ended with a wonderful discharge of fireworks, rockets, wheels, and detonating stars.

Much glory to the boys and girls; but glory earned by weeks of earnest work.

Enter one of the primary schools, from which these children swarm into the streets. A goodly edifice—clean stairs and passages—silence like the hush of summer woods—a door that opens to a touch—a teacher glad to see you enter—children at their desks, and evidently used to strangers coming in and going out—these things strike the senses first. You look around the class-room, which contains some fifty boys, from six or seven to nine or ten years old. These lads are all so clean and spruce, that you are tempted to exclaim, 'Are these your city Arabs?' In Geneva, lying close to Savoy, there are many poor, and some neglected people. Standing at the outlet of three Alpine valleys, she receives into her streets the overflow from Sallanche, from Annecy, from St. Claude; and if her streets are not so littered with the waste of life as those of Lyons, there are some undoubted Arabs here and there about her cafés and along her quays.

'Our city Arabs,' says the teacher, 'drop their nature when they come to school. Our laws are strict, and we enforce them with the utmost zeal. Our law declares that every child has a right to come to school; and his exclusion from the school is felt to be a serious blow for him. We punish, therefore, by refusing him his seat. At six, a boy should come to us of right, and claim his place; but we retain by law a power to strip him of that right. We use this power in cases where the child is not in fault, but where the public good requires a sacrifice of private right—as where a child is either deaf, dumb, blind, or idiotic. Children who have not been vaccinated, children who are suffering from diseases, children who present disfigured and repulsive faces, are excluded. After they have got their seats, they may be sent away for bad behaviour in the school, and on the way to school. A child is made to feel that coming to the school is like the going to a palace and a church.'

'But some of them must come in filth and rags?'

'Yes, some; not many and not long. For dirt is but a habit of the eye, and habits of the eye are quickly changed. We wash the dirty ones, and send them home with shining skins. A mother gets ashamed on finding that some other woman has to wash her child. The child, too, gets ashamed; for all the little lads about him are as clean as new-shelled peas. No boy has ever to be washed three times.'

A stranger's eye can see scant difference in the scholars as to class, since all are trim and tight, and look well fed.

'Is there much mixture of the various social classes in your Primary Schools?'

'We have no social classes in our commonwealth.'

'Of course not. Pardon me. But you have offices and professions, like the outer world. You have, for instance, Councillors of State. Are any of your boys the sons of Councillors of State?'

'I cannot say so. In some Cantons, such as Bern and Zürich, you will find the son of a professor sitting in a primary school with sons of weavers, goatherds, and mechanics. In Geneva it is not the mode. We Latins are democratic in our speeches, and Geneva is to us the centre of all liberal thought; but not one member of the democratic party in Geneva will allow his boy to mix with common lads. You think he would deny this statement? You are right, he would deny it; yet he does not send his Jean and Henri to the primary school.'

Inquiry proves this teacher to be right in what he says about the freer mixture of all classes in Teutonic Cantons.

'Your pupils come from every grade?' I ask a Zürich teacher.

'Yes,' he answers, 'every grade. This boy

is a professor's son. You know his father. He is B——. The next to him—that clever-looking lad—is a cabman's son.'

'Professor B—— has no objection to his boy being school-mate to the cabman's son?'

'No, none. Why should he have? In countries where you have a privileged class such things may be. With us ability is the only rank, and men are thrown together in their later life according to the groups they form at school. If A. is equal to B. in learning, he is equal to him in everything that ought to count.'

I take the actual census in one Zürich class. The boys are fifty-two in number, and their ages seven to eight.

Sons of shopkeepers		21
,,	merchants	10
,,	petty tradesmen	4
,,	innkeepers	4
,,	professors	2
Son of a musician		1
,,	an apothecary	1
,,	an architect	1
,,	a business agent	1
,,	a porter	1
,,	a day labourer	1
,,	a clothes-cleaner	1
Unclassified		4
		52

In talking on this subject to Professor B——, I find the teacher right in substance even when he errs in form. Professor B—— does not exactly hold that learning gives the only title to respect; he thinks that gentle manners and a manly spirit count for something; but he sees that in a free commonwealth, where power depends on popularity, it is the best thing for a lad that he should grow up with his fellows. 'Mark me,' also adds Professor B——, 'the education that my boy obtains in the public school is very good, and is provided for him at the public cost.'

In the Teutonic Cantons, though the teaching is not better, there is less division of society in the schools. The Teutons talk much less about equality than the Latins; but the Teutons practise, while the Latins only preach. A Councillor of State in such a Canton as Geneva is an aristocrat in feeling, though a democrat in flag. He keeps a shop (say) on the Grand Quay; he owns a villa on the lake; he has a room of books, a cabinet of wines. He takes an interest in this question of primary instruction. Only yesterday he spoke for upwards of an hour in answer to Professor Vogt; his eyes aglow with light; his tones impressed with zeal; his passion noble, tender, liberal; yet he sees no need to let his children mix with those of citizens A. and B., who vend their wares in smaller streets, and are not Councillors of State. His fellows in the Council send their boys to private schools, and he must send his also to a private school.

'Do tradesmen send their children to you?'

'Yes; the greater part. The school is good, and cheap. No private master can pretend to vie with us. What *he* can offer is exclusiveness —a dear and poor instruction, in a smaller house and a less airy place. A man has not yet come to be a true republican if he prefers a private to a public school. The higher class of tradesmen send their sons, and these good fellows are our Attic salt.'

'Your walls and floors and desks are very clean. Your passages and staircase show no scratch and scrawl. No bits of paper dot the floors, no splash of ink defaces desk and form.'

'Our discipline is one of self-respect and self-restraint. We teach our children how to think and act, no less than how to read and write. Instruction is but part of education. If our plans are right, it is in fact the lesser part. We pay as much attention to the things of life as to the things of learning. Thus we see to a boy's manners and appearance: how he looks, and how he walks, and how he speaks. We see that he has washed his hands, and that he keeps his papers clean. We teach him to regard a blot upon his page as worse than even a smudge upon his face. A book befouled with grime is wasted, and our simple habits will not suffer waste. Turn over any of these books—the books in daily use—no leaf is torn, no cover is defaced. The writing-desk, though ink is freely used, is free from speck and spot.'

'Your boys seem gentle to the touch; but you must have some rougher types of lad? What means have you of keeping the unruly spirits in such order?'

'We expel them. Such a case is rare; in some schools hardly known. A threat suffices to subdue the proudest flesh. In truth, to be expelled from school is only one degree from ruin. Where can the expelled one go? Our laws about exchange of school are very strict. These laws permit a lad whose parent passes from one village to another to exchange his school, but recognise no other cause as giving him a natural right to change. Nor can such change be made at all without a special leave, in writing, from the inspector of his district school. A special leave is hard to get. Thus change is rare, and when it comes the cause of it is known; and so a lad who is expelled must go into a second school with evil name and fame. His course in that new place will not be smooth.'

'Expulsion is with you a public act?'

'Entirely so—that is, expulsion in the last degree.'

'You have degrees?'

'Yes, three degrees; a first, a second, and a third degree. The first is a forbidding of the school; it may be for a day, a week; and when the lad returns his parents must come with him, and must promise he shall mend his ways. The second is removal for a longer term; a month, a quarter, perhaps; when he can only take his place again by an express authority from either the inspector of his district or his village mayor. The third expulsion is the last. It is a public act. The master and inspector must consent; the Educational Department must concur. No boy can be expelled from school excepting by this public act.'

'Expulsion is your last resource; but you have other means?'

'Yes; many.'

'Of a moral kind? Your laws, I think, prohibit every form of corporal punishment?'

'Our laws are clear upon that point. No bodily pain, no bodily shame, is suffered in our schools. A lad has rights. We cannot stint his food; we cannot lock him up; we cannot put him in a corner; we cannot lay him on his back; we cannot crown him with a dunce's cap; we cannot make a guy of him, even though his parents should request us to employ such means.'

'Your discipline is wholly moral?'

'Yes; our means are prizes—smiles, good words, good notes; all leading up to public acts of honour, when the more deserving pupils are the heroes of their time. Desire to win a prize has more effect than fear of punishment in keeping scholars out of mischief. Pranks take time, and boys who mean to win their prizes have no time to spare.'

'But now and then some boy offends the rule?'

'A word, a glance, a call of name, suffice in almost every case. We sometimes have to keep a lad an hour in school, when all his fellows have gone home. We sometimes give an extra task to learn. We mark his card; we let his parents know of his default. In some bad cases, we may keep him in a room apart. If all these methods fail—and they but seldom fail—we may expel him for a week, a month; and in the last resort we turn him out of school for good and bad.'

'You never use the rod?'

'The law does not permit us.'

'But you have a rod; it seems much worn about the end?'

'We point with it; and beat the desk with it; and—yes—we sometimes touch a dull boy's fingers with it.'

'Do you ever box a lad's ears?'

'Well, no; I hardly think so. Not in anger, surely; we may tickle him by a little slap, but not to hurt him; just to wake him up. Our discipline is that of steady, daily work. Our youngsters have no idle hours. We have abolished mischief with the penalties for mischief. Look at our Scheme of Work, and tell me how a lad who has to face it can indulge in prank and play.'

CHAPTER XXVIII.

SCHEME OF WORK.

These Genevese lads are seven years old and upwards. Most of them are eight or ten.

A few have been at infant-schools. The state encourages such schools, and helps them by a public grant; but Communes are not forced to found them, and in many Cantons infant-schools are hardly known. The few who may have been at infant-schools have learnt to count, to name their letters, both in type and writing, and to sing their baby songs. All that was play—the time has come for work.

Each child must stay six years at school, and every year, if he does well, should see him mount his ladder step by step. For every year there is a new degree.

First Degree.

The infant stage is past, and in the outset

every lad is thought to know as much as would be taught him at an infant-school. The first degree is that of reading, writing, and accounting. He has to undergo a course of pictures on the wall, with object lessons on the different themes. He learns to read and spell a little, and he makes his first acquaintance with a book—a simple spelling-book. He now begins to write—to copy hooks, rings, strokes, and bars; to study letters, in the capital form; and afterwards to set down, from dictation of his master, letters, syllables, and easy words. In arithmetic he studies adding and subtracting only. He must copy numbers up to twenty. He must know the figures both by ear and eye, and practise writing them by sound and sight. He learns addition and subtraction up to twenty. In this early stage the singing is of simple sort, and not so much a lesson as a game.

Second Degree.

The lessons open with an exercise on moral life, on natural history, on the laws of health, and on historical events. These exercises are to be continued by the master, in all after years, up to the sixth degree. The reading is expected to be better, care being given to an exact pronunciation of the words. The writing goes from big to middle size, and when the figures grow more easy to the child, he is allowed to try the finer forms. In his arithmetic he makes a stride; he numbers, adds, subtracts up to a thousand; reckons by the mind, and makes acquaintance with his second book—a treatise on addition and subtraction. As he marks his way, the master gives him some examples of multiplication as they stand connected with the rules of addition, now familiar to his eye. A new and most important study stands before him—French, his native speech. He has to learn some words each day by heart; to study, copy, and dictate these words. He hears of noun, verb, article, and adjective, and tries to master how these parts of speech are used. He gets some lessons on gender and number; and continues singing, as before.

Third Degree.

In the third degree (besides the exercises on moral life, on natural history, on laws of health, and on historical events) the lad is taught to read a current page, and then the master tells him what it means. Great care is paid to pronunciation; and the teacher must explain the use of dashes, dots, and hyphens, on a page of print. The writing is continued in all hands—the big, the medium, and the fine. Examples must be written out. The cyphering must include addition, subtraction, and multiplication, up to any number, with study of the works on these three operations. Simple cases of division, as developed from subtraction, may be given, with problems and exercises of a simple kind. The French is more advanced; the lad is told to use a vocabulary; and up to this date—a boy's third year at school—it is supposed that he has never seen a book of words! He is now to tackle time and person—in his grammar; and his master is to tell him of indicative and imperative, gender and number, subject and object. He is taught the formation of plurals, and to know a personal pronoun when he sees it. He is introduced to feminine and masculine, and taught to see the kinship of an adjective and a verb. He has to face another subject, drawing, which he first encounters in the shape of lines and angles; but he only has to face it for an hour a week, and with a rule and compass in his hand. His singing lessons still go on.

Fourth Degree.

Exercises on morals, natural history, and laws of health, as usual, current reading, with an explanation; also dashes, dots, and hyphens as before. The reading lessons now include intonation; study and recital of simple pieces; with questions and replies. The writing is after model and dictation, with copies of invoices and bills. The cyphering includes multiplication and division up to any numbers. The French becomes more complex: studies in the construction of co-ordinate propositions, auxiliary verbs, the commoner class of irregular verbs, the passive form, and explanations of the adverb, preposition, and conjunction. Learning of words by heart goes on. The drawing must advance some steps. No rule, no compass is allowed; a printed model is hung up; and all the pupils copy it as they can. When single lines and angles have been neatly done, a pupil is instructed to combine them into groups. Another subject has been introduced this year—geography; this subject for two hours a-week. Geography is taught on natural lines; the teacher starts with Geneva, and explains from what is known by sight to what is only known by word. Land and water lead to continent and ocean, and the general features of the earth's surface are exhibited in lake and alp.

The singing has become more serious, and a goodly slice of time is now given up to exercise and drill.

Fifth Degree.

Exercise and current reading as before, but more of it. More singing, exercise, and drill than ever.

The reading lessons are continued, with explanations, questions, and replies. Much time is given to intonation, also to reading poetry and selected bits of prose aloud. The writing lessons take the form of copying models, and writing under dictation. In his fifth year the pupil commences round hand, of the sort which English boys learn first and then forget. The cyphering begins with practice in the four rules, separately and conjointly, then proceeds to decimal fractions and the four operations in decimals. Practice continues; mental arithmetic continues; and the pupils dash at vulgar fractions. French progresses into the abstruser parts of grammar; and the lessons are on the different sorts of determinatives, the chief exceptions to the formation of plural and feminine, the classification of pronouns, the conjugation of verbs, the preposition and the adverb. Exercises in analysis are given. The drawing now includes the outlines of seas and continents, together with such figures as consist of straight lines and curves only. Outline maps are made. The geography takes in the world; the lessons being three—a general view of the five parts of the globe, a special view of Europe, and a fuller view of Switzerland in her physical aspects. Two fresh subjects have been introduced this year—geometry and history. In the class of geometry the pupil studies lines, angles, figures, with the measurement of plain surfaces. The history is local, following the plan pursued in the class of geography, and sets before the boy a picture of his country from the earliest to the latest times.

Sixth Degree.

Not to speak of exercises in morals, natural history, the laws of health, and historical events; not to speak of current readings, with an explanation of the use of hyphen, dot, and dash; the subjects in the sixth degree are eight in number, without counting music, exercise, and drill.

These eight subjects are severely taught; the lads being twelve years old.

The reading now consists of exercises in intonation and declamation; summaries by voice and writing; special treatises on history, health, natural history, agriculture (for the country folk), and science as applied to industry for all; and recitations of poetry and selected bits of prose.

The writing now embraces cursive hand under dictation, models of round hand, copies of public acts, of bills, of letters on business, with specimens in all the styles, big, middling, cursive, round. The arithmetic comprises sums in vulgar fractions, in mixed numbers, some ideas of aliquot parts, the metrical system, the rule of three and application of this rule to interests, discounts, dividends. The French embraces lessons on invariable words, the principal exceptions to the rules of concord, the participles, the collective nouns, the main difficulties of French syntax. These are followed by a string of exercises; exercises on the modification which changes in the verb cause the prepositions; on the general principles of composition, on the rules of epistolary correspondence; on common synonymes; on bad grammar and on slang. The drawing passes from even lines and curves into the representation of common objects, houses, men, and boats, and the master gives instruction in perspective, and in light and shade. Objects are copied and models made. The class of geometry employs itself upon the means of measuring surfaces and bodies, with the art and practice of surveying land. Three hours a-week are given to geography; including, first, a detailed study of Switzerland and the adjacent parts of Savoy, Burgundy, and Franche Comté; second, lessons on the form and motion of the earth; third, a general view of the starry heavens. The history consists of courses on national events from 1513 (the first year of the Republic) to 1848 (when the existing system of Confederate Cantons took its form), the constitution of Geneva, and the Federal pact.

An extra subject—that of agriculture—is taught in the country schools. A master parts his sixth year into agricultural sessions; in the first of which he gives instruction on the nature of soils, the different kinds of soil, the art of mixing and manuring soil, together with the use and economy of labour; in the second, he discourses on agricultural implements, on seeds and dried plants, on various cereals, vines, straw, forage, and the like, with hints on noxious plants and animals, on insects, and the general business of a husbandman.

To this large list of subjects must be added singing and gymnastics, branches of primary education which are given in two divisions, and in unison with each other. Both are taught with care, and both with reference to a due development of the physical and the moral powers.

These pupils in Geneva toil more hours a-year than any one would like to set our boys to toil. A school week in Geneva numbers thirty hours; a year from forty-four to forty-six weeks. These hours and weeks are those in which the pupil must attend at school; but they are only half the time he is expected to be hard at work. This rule is matter of the strictest law. 'All scholars in the primary schools have daily tasks to do at home; the length and value of which tasks are in proportion to their age.' In rural districts some discretion is allowed the teacher in this matter. Lads of seven or eight may be exempted from these tasks; but no such weakness is displayed in towns. The task at home is nearly equal to the task at school. Inquiry at Geneva and Lausanne has shown me that the hours of study —school-work, drill, and home-work—are not less than ten, and often rise as high as twelve or thirteen hours a-day. In fine, these Switzers tug at learning as we English tug at trade.

CHAPTER XXIX.

SECONDARY SCHOOLS.

A LAD who passes through his six degrees, and through his extra subjects, in a primary school, with fair success, is not unfit to enter on his course of active life in any of the lower grades. He may aspire to drive a coach, to row a boat, to fell a wood, to guide a plough. His age is only twelve; the world is all before him; and more paths than one entice his feet. If he would keep what he has got, and clutch at more, an evening school is open either in his village or a neighbouring village, where, his daily toil being ended, he may follow science to her secret haunts. In evening schools the course of study runs to three full years; the masters are the best that can be hired; the mayor and councillors take an interest in them; and a lad who keeps his terms, and finishes his course, will then have had the benefit of being under good instruction for at least nine years. He ought to know his subjects well.

If he should aim at higher things, and if his parents can afford to spare him in the early hours, he goes into a secondary school. A country lad, he finds his secondary school in either his native village or a neighbouring village, always at an easy walk from home. A city lad, he finds his secondary school in the shape of either a college or a special school; but always in a neighbouring street. The means are at his door; and if he fails to use them, it is not the public fault.

All public schools for secondary teaching in the Canton of Geneva may be grouped under two heads: the rural schools, the city schools; each group of institutions framed to meet the wants of those who come to them. The country schools are mostly union schools. One Commune only—that of Satigny—has a secondary school for itself. In one case, two Communes—Meyrin and Vernier—have a school between them. Generally four Communes join in keeping up a secondary school. The forty-two Communes in the Canton of Geneva have twelve of these rural schools among them.

A lad begins his second education at the point where he broke off his first. In entering on his thirteenth year, he finds in front of him three years of toil. A part of these arrangements stands the same for boys and girls: to wit, the principles of moral science; French, with composition and the elements of style; elocution; the more important facts in modern history, with reference to the history of Geneva; common geography, with the use of globes; meteorology; the elements of physic, natural history, and chemistry; the laws of health; the art of writing; singing. Here lines divide, and the instruction is adapted to the sex. A separate course is given to boys, on civic duties, on geometry applied to measurements, on agricultural science, on the books for a farm; and exercises are provided in drawing common objects, in gymnastics, and in German—if the regent is able to teach this language. Girls are taught in special classes, how to cast accounts, to tend plants and flowers, to use the needle, and to keep the house. The girls are also taught the art of treating sick and wounded men.

One school suffices for both girls and boys; the boys attending only in the morning, while the girls come only in the afternoon. This suits the parents, who could hardly spare their children all at once from work; and makes one schoolhouse serve for both the sexes. A regent has the general charge. A quarter of the regent's salary is paid by the united Communes, three-quarters by the Canton. In return these secondary schools are founded when and where the Council of State sees fit.

The elements of drill begin the very first week of a scholar's course. A teacher sets his pupils in a row; he makes them stand erect; he moves their limbs together; bids them bend, recover, stretch the hands, march, leap, and jump. All kinds of games are practised in the play-ground. Every game that tends to open and expand the chest, to nerve the limbs, and give a carriage to the frame, is studied, and, if need be, introduced. From six to eight a lad is exercised in simple motions of the body; at the age of nine he learns to hold a pole, to run with ropes, and swing on bars. From ten to thirteen harder things—made easy by the previous training—are commenced. The lines are formed like regular squads; the exercise is but another name for drill. In walking, running, hopping, every one obeys the word; whirls, changes front, and halts as he is told. All exercise is orderly and rhythmical. Much care is taken with the halting, turning round, and facing to the right or left. The squads are put through many exercises in bending, twisting, reaching, and recovering at the ease. Long jumps and high jumps, every sort of sport on foot, with hanging by the hands and feet from rungs, with climbing poles and ropes, with bounding from a spring-board, and a hundred games that strengthen, temper, and adjust the frame.

On leaving one of these rural schools at fifteen years of age, a lad is fit for any post that he is likely to obtain; is fit to be a waiter, farmer, boatman, forester, and so on; and is also fit to exercise his public rights—to hold his rifle and to cast his vote. For such a lad can read and write, can sing and shoot; he knows the constitution of his country, and can follow with a free intelligence the politics of his city and his State. Of course he is no scholar, for he knows no Greek and Latin, and his range of language, poetry, mythology, and humanities, is not wide. He has no chance of entering the professions. He cannot hope to be an advocate, physician, clergyman, professor. If he means to try a higher flight, he must repair to one of the burgher schools.

The burgher schools in the Canton of Geneva — which may be taken as examples of their fellows are: (1) the College of Geneva; (2) the College of Carouge; (3) the Industrial and Commercial School; (4) the Supplementary School; (5) the Superior Ladies' School.

Pupils, whether boys or girls, are subject to preliminary examination, in the presence of certain persons named by the Department of Public Instruction. These examinations are very strict, alike for scholars who have passed through public schools and private schools. Some general rules apply to each and all. No class can be increased beyond sixty pupils; the year comprises forty weeks at least; the hours of study in each week are fixed at thirty in summer time, at thirty-two in winter time; examination in the several branches must be holden once a-year at least; and a festival of promotion is given at the conclusion of the summer term.

The most renowned of these superior schools is the College of Geneva. If our aspirant is a city lad, ambition will induce him to prefer that school. It is divided into two main sections—a classical section, a commercial section; and the boy will enter one or other, as his aim in life suggests. He studies to some end, and takes his course according to that end.

The course of classical education runs seven years—from the age of fifteen to twenty-two. The course includes—the principles of morality; French, with composition and the elements of style; the art of making verses; diction; Latin, Greek, mythology (clubbed together as one subject); the German language; the salient points of general history and national history; the rights and duties of a citizen; ancient and modern geography; arithmetic; caligraphy; singing; and gymnastics. All these subjects must be taught; but extra subjects may be introduced, if they are not allowed to interfere with what the law lays down as fixed and regular work. An English eye sees much to note as odd in such a list of subjects. How can composition be regarded as a separate study from versification, and, still more, from diction? How can Latin, Greek, and Mythology, be treated in a single class? No English master dreams of giving lessons on the rights and duties of a citizen. What public school in England teaches writing as an art? Yet most of these things seem so natural to a Switzer, that he starts when you remark upon them. All French teachers pay attention to their native tongue, and dwell, with an adoring fondness, on its beauty, force, and point. We give our youth to Latin, and a Latin gives his youth to French. The rights and duties of a citizen are themes of daily interest to a Switzer, who must take his part in every movement of the state. A country squire in England likes his son to know a little law, for he may have to judge offenders from the local bench. All Switzers may have magisterial duties to discharge—as village mayor, as justice of the peace, as councillor of state; and thus the rights and duties of a citizen are taught in all the secondary and superior schools. That caligraphy should be studied as a separate branch, by youths of twenty-two, may seem absurd; but the result is good; and nearly all these Switzers write in hands which men who run may read. One knows some English hands— and those of men the best worth reading—which no mortal patience can make out. A young man who has kept his seven years in the classical section of this college should be fit for most things in his Canton — short of a professor's chair.

The commercial section differs from the classical section in the length and course of study. Six instead of seven years complete the series, and the Greek and Latin tongues give place to English. Every care is given to practical training for office. The course of study runs — morals; French, with composition, elements of style, and literary history; diction; the German tongue; the English tongue for the superior classes; salient points of general history and national history; the rights and duties of a citizen; mythology; geography, and cosmography; the history of discoveries; a brief history of the arts; elements of political economy; arithmetic; book-keeping; elementary algebra, with logarithms; elementary geometry and trigonometry, with application to topography; the elements of physics and mechanics; studies in natural history and chemistry; drawing, with descriptive geometry; caligraphy; singing; gymnastics.

At the end of these two courses — at the age of twenty-two and twenty-one respectively — the pupils who have passed a satisfactory examination receive certificates of capacity, and may then proceed to any university and so prepare themselves for the bar, the pulpit, the professor's chair.

The College of Carouge—intended mainly for the Catholic population, who are less instructed, as a rule, than the Calvinistic population—has a course of three years only; corresponding to the first three years in the College of Geneva. Carouge is separated from Geneva by a mile of neutral territory, called the Plain; but what a difference in the people and the schools! Carouge is Savoyard, not Swiss. Adjoined to the republic of Geneva, in 1814, for political reasons by the Powers, this town has none of the traditions of Geneva, and her people rank among the least enlightened members of the League. Laws which suit the Free City do not suit this Catholic suburb. Every rule must be relaxed. The term from six or seven years to three is lowered. The hours demanded in the week are fewer. They may be only twenty-six; and they are mostly twenty-six. A lad who passes through this college of Carouge is not prepared to enter on a higher course of study, and he cannot hope to win professional rank.

Here lies the secret of that high predominance which the Calvinistic population of the city exercises over the Catholic population of the country, even in the face of a majority of Catholic votes. If ruling force in a republic lay in numbers only, and the march of public law was governed by the polling-booth, this Canton of Geneva should be ultramontane, like the Catholic bishop, Gaspard Mermillod, who rules, as Curé of Geneva, an unruly flock of sheep. The latest census gives the several confessions in the Canton thus:

Catholics	48,340 souls.
Evangelicals	44,138 ,,
Jews	1,001 ,,
Other Sects	637 ,,

Mermillod, therefore, has a clear and strong majority of the Canton at his back. The suffrage is universal; and a clear majority in the polling-booths should give him a majority in the Hôtel de Ville. But he has no such power; the better taught minority carries everything before it in the public council and the public press.

CHAPTER XXX.

SCHOOL AND CAMP.

DIRECTOR Max Wirth of Bern assures me that no boy, no girl, exists in this Confederation—save an idiot here and there—who cannot read and write. So far as one can judge, Herr Wirth is right, as to the outer side of things. All Switzers seem to be—and to have been—at school. There must be some exceptions to this happy rule; exceptions in remote and barren wilds, where nature gives her offspring an embrace like that of wolves and bears. In cities there are no illiterate classes like the savages of London, Paris, and New York; but in such chasms as break the snowy alps of Schwyz and Uri, where the pine and larch can hardly grasp the rocks, there may be found some unkempt, untaught boors. Not many, perhaps—but some; enough to show that men are men, and that the sternest rules may fail where nature works against them. More than once, in crossing by the passes of Graubünden, through the Fore Rhine country, I have come on village schools shut up; and on inquiring at the nearest house of call, have learned that that they are closed for more than six months out of twelve. In summer time a lad is on the mountains tending goats; in winter time his house is buried under snow. The school is three miles from his door; how can he be expected to attend it every day? The law may tell him he must go to school. The law sounds well enough in Chur; but who shall fetch him from the Alpine tops, and who unearth him from the falling snow? In these secluded mountain troughs the life is hard, the priest is easy, and the village mayor is kind. A peasant mayor can feel for peasant woes; and though he reads the law, and talks of putting it in force from day to day, the months slip by, and Johann is not seen at school. But these exceptions hardly tell against the mass. In looking broadly for results, these Alpine savages may well be dropped. 'We reckon all such waifs and strays as idiots,' Wirth remarks. They need not mar the picture, though they shade it with a little cloud.

In general terms, all Switzers, male and female, may be said to read and write, to keep accounts, to sing, to shoot, and take a personal and intelligent part in what concerns the public weal.

How much unlike the state of things in England, who shall need to say? At home, we English stand outside the lists; and even in the United States our kinsmen show to disadvantage. Take the census of 1860 in the United States. The figures will astound some persons who have long been saying that if education is neglected on the parent soil, it flourishes abundantly among our sons. How stands the record? In America the number of illiterate men and women, white of skin, and over twenty-one years old, is upwards of a million. The number of illiterate persons is increasing, not diminishing. In 1840 the white-skins over twenty-one who could not read and write were 549,850; in 1850 these illiterates had increased to 962,898; in 1860 they had swelled to 1,126,575. If you were to throw in other classes—red-skins, black-skins, yellow-skins—you would increase this number very much. The yellow-skins and red-skins were not counted in this census, but the black-skins were; and from this colour only the Department of Education add 1,750,536 adults to the mass of ignorant whites. In all, the States report that they are burthened with a population of 2,872,111 whites and blacks who neither read nor write.

Thus the number of ignorant adults in America — of men who read no books, no laws, no constitutions, no reports, yet exercise political power — is greater than the whole population of Switzerland. It may be fancied that these ignorant whites are strangers; this is partly true, though not to any large extent. The mass of those who neither read nor write are natives of the soil. We cite these figures from the census:—

Illiterate white adults, 1860:
    Native-born 871,418
    Foreign-born 346,893

But some may dream that this neglect of education in America is partial only; in the ignorant South, in the chaotic West. The tables yield no facts that would support this view. What strikes one most in going through these tables is the uniformity of ignorance in the leading States. Virginia—home of Chivalry—is the most ignorant State of all; but North Carolina and Tennessee are not far behind. Read this tale of grown-up white men and women who (in 1860) could neither read nor write:—

In the State of Virginia	. . .	72,000 souls.
,,	North Carolina . .	68,000 ,,
,,	Tennessee . .	67,000 ,,
,,	Kentucky . .	63,000 ,,
,,	Indiana . .	54,000 ,,
,,	Ohio . . .	41,000 ,,
,,	Illinois . .	38,000 ,,
,,	Pennsylvania . .	36,000 ,,
,,	New York . .	20,000 ,,

Horace Mann asserts that these returns are far below the facts. He takes some pains to show that many persons are returned as able to read and write who are not able; and he adds no less than forty in the hundred to these numbers, in correction of that false return. He nearly doubles the enormous totals of these ignorant whites.

Select one State for more exact comparison with Switzerland. Take Pennsylvania as a special State, in which the care of education has been constant, from the day when Sydney aided Penn to frame a true Republican constitution. The population of Pennsylvania is a little over that of Switzerland. The State has 13,936 schools, with 815,763 pupils attending them, yet the number of men and women, white of skin, and over twenty-one years old, who cannot read and write, stands in the latest census at 36,000! The school law of Pennsylvania dates from 1848, about the time when Switzerland began her educational reform. But many of the townships would not execute the law. A sect who call themselves Economists oppose the State department, and in 1860, when the tables were compared, these ignorant brethren still controlled results. In Switzerland the townships have no power to question and postpone the law. These facts and figures on America are taken from a report of the Commissioner of Education, dated Washington, Oct. 27, 1870, and that Commissioner, Mr. Eaton, has the duty of correcting them if they are wrong. My end in citing them is to suggest, on both sides of the Ocean, what a task is still before us, ere we English get in line with these keen dwellers on the alps.

The cost at which these great results are purchased by the Switzers, is, for them, immense; but education is their chief affair; the cost of education stands in nearly all the Cantonal budgets even before the army, though that army is the national force. The totals for these services in 1870:—

Cost of Cantonal troops . . . 4,508,901 frs.
  ,,   ,,   schools . . . 5,157,756

Such figures are so startling, in comparison with budgets like our own, that one is tempted to extract these details from the tables kept in Bern:—

Cost of Cantonal Schools and Armies.

CANTON.	SCHOOL.	ARMY.
1. Zürich	881,804 frs.	516,449 frs.
2. Bern	1,076,558	858,839
3. Luzern	201,168	212,485
4. Uri	12,106	20,947
5. Schwyz	14,266	34,886
6. Unterwalden	11,594	23,225
7. Glarus	14,789	52,337
8. Zug	12,652	18,805
9. Freiburg	160,683	168,497
10. Solothurn	101,630	145,008
11. Basel	455,790	164,450
12. Schaffhausen	109,284	77,084
13. Appenzell	51,315	80,531
14. St. Gallen	167,586	326,593
15. Graubünden	104,127	153.017
16. Aargau	500,668	334,290
17. Thurgau	131,048	117,575
18. Ticino	122,076	111,093
19. Vaud	398,597	562,170
20. Valais	37,503	146,910
21. Neufchatel	177,097	150,874
22. Geneva	335,445	227,840
Totals	5,157,756	4,508,901

These figures show the cost for schools and troops so far as the expense is charged upon the Cantonal budgets, and are safe for contrast just so far as they extend. Three other items lie outside :—(1) The amount contributed by each Commune in support of its own primary schools; (2) the amount contributed by the League in support of the Polytechnic ; (3) the amount contributed by the League in support of the Federal army. When the first and second of these items have been added to the cost of schools, the bill stands thus :—

Cost of Communal schools . . . 5,000,000 frs.
,, Cantonal schools . . . 5,157,756
,, Federal school (Polytechnic) . . 287,611
10,445,367

I give the round figure of five million francs as the cost of Communal schools on the authority of Herr Wirth. It is the lowest sum that can be named. When the third item is added to the cost of war, the bill stands thus :—

Cost of Cantonal troops . . . 4,508,901 frs.
,, Federal troops . . . 5,486,396
9,995,297

Thus we have it proved, and in official papers, that in Switzerland more money is expended on the public schools than on the public forces. Such a fact is sought in vain elsewhere. In

London, Paris, and Berlin, war budgets come in great excess of education budgets; eight, ten, twelve to one, it may be. Look at these totals, put into English money:—

Cost of Swiss schools	£417,814
„ Swiss army	399,811

Yet in Switzerland every man is drilled and armed, and ready to turn out and fight. Here lies the secret of a cheap defence.

The truth is that a soldier learns his business in the school; not only exercise and drill, the use of arms, the habits of obedience, order, silence, cleanliness, the power to listen and to speak; but those yet higher duties of a camp, the will to mingle class with class, to act in bodies with a single soul, to put down personal hopes and fears, and seek no object but the public good. 'We have to guard the refuge,' says a Federal colonel,—as we quit the military school at Thun, where we have seen the Cantonal officers at their tasks—'our forces are but slight; our only strength is that derived from mutual help. Your rivalries and struggles would not suit us; for our schools are but the opening to a camp where every man must take his place and find his brethren in the rank and file. You see we are a handful in the midst of powerful nations. How could we maintain our own unless we put forth all our forces ? How are we to get from each and all the utmost measure of his strength ?'

'The answer to that question is the secret of your public life.'

'My answer is,—we get it through the class-room and the drill-ground. In the school we melt our crude metallic ores ; and in the camp we fuse them into bronze.'

x

CHAPTER XXXI.

DEFENCE.

No armed men are seen about the streets. From Basel to Bellinzona, from Carouge to Rorschach, you may drive through every Canton of the League, and hardly meet one soldier on the road. It is not so around you; for in every frontier city you encounter men with belt and rifle — bright and brisk in one place, low and loafing in another—but in every frontier town you find imperial, royal, and republican bands. Bregenz is full of Austrian troops; Constanz is full of German troops; Como is full of Italian troops; Belfort is full of French troops. Out, on every side of her, the nations are in arms; in open and professional array of force; and ready, as they seem, to take the field. She looks defenceless in the centre of this ring of camps. The only folk you see in these free Cantons clothed in uniforms are students coming from the public schools.

And yet this League of free republics is not unprepared for war.

You find no soldiers in the streets, because these Cantons have no separate military class; but every man you see in shop and field would start into a soldier if his bugle called; a soldier, armed, equipped, and ready for the march. The groom who feeds your horse may be a corporal; the doctor who prepares your draught may be a captain of the line. No power is wasted by these Cantons. Every man is trained to face his duties when the trumpet sounds.

Come with me to a Cantonal drill-ground; that of Zürich, for example. In a broad, green meadow, called the Wollis Hofen, lying at the foot of Uetliberg, the boys of Zürich drill and shoot on summer days. This meadow is an ancient river-bed, now soft and grassy, with a ridge of ground about it, shutting off the lake; four miles in distance from the Polytechnic and the Cantonal schools. Hither march the boys on certain days with pipe and drum, with glittering steel and mounted guns; the linesmen carrying rifles, the artillery wearing swords. Some companies of Cantonal troops are in advance; going out to practise at the range.

A group of teachers and professors—men whose names are known to Europe—Kinkel, Vögelin, and Behn-Eschenburg—are with the boys, and will be followed, later in the day, by groups of parents, sisters, and it may be sweet-hearts; ready with their cheering cries and waving hands, to mark each movement in the field. Arrived at Wollis Hofen, the procession halts, a line is formed, the names are called, the arms and uniforms are noted, and the several companies told off to drill and shoot.

A little drill suffices for the younger fry; who march, and wheel, and skirmish, and are then dismissed for play. But play itself is part of drill. These youngsters race and leap, and throw the ball, and try to catch their comrades in a coil of rope. Two swords are stuck into the ground as barriers, and the urchins chase each other round these shining points.

More work is given to boys of riper age; the full battalion drill, and firing, company by company, at a range of butts. A volunteer myself, I note with care the doings of these lads, and find in them a good deal to approve; though much of it is better for the field than for parade. The wheeling is a little loose; the line is sometimes bent; and here and there a lad falls out of step. But these are faults of that loose system which the Zürichers have borrowed from the French. The skirmishing is quick and steady; the recovery into line alert. Still better is the firing at a mark. I should not like to be a Zouave clambering up a rock with one of these young marksmen of fifteen behind the ledge.

A park of guns is on the ground. The Cantonal school-boys form the line; the Polytechnic students serve the guns. Except that many of the lads wear glasses, they have very much the look of youths who will be soldiers by-and-by. A canteen is erected on the meadow, but no sign of drink being close at hand is seen. A thin, red wine is sold to such as want it; but the boys prefer their grapes and apples — fruit of which they seem to have abundant crops. One corner of the meadow is enlivened by a band, round which the ladies and professors sit; and at the butts a rifle-match is on between two Cantonal shooting clubs. The boys observe this shooting with intense delight; a cry of rapture greets each score; and men of every age—from eight to eighty, and of every rank—from labourers to professors — stand together on this Zürich drill-ground, foot to foot, and wrist to wrist, as one may say, in the freemasonry of arms.

Some cheap and homely prizes — canes, and drinking-mugs, and albums — are distributed by a city magistrate to such as have done well. The band strikes up the 'Rhine Watch,' and the youngsters shout hurrah, and toss their caps into the sky. A great professor speaks a few warm words, and then the business of the day is done. A bugle calls, the companies fall in, and homeward march begins. Half Zürich comes to greet us on the quays and in the streets, and having spent ten hours in the open fields, we all feel ready for a frugal supper and a dreamless sleep.

In every Canton of the League you find such schools of arms as that of Wollis Hofen; drill and shooting grounds belonging to the State, and reckoned as the necessary adjuncts of a public school. For with a Switzer drill begins as soon as he can stand erect and poise a stick. In many Cantons drill begins at six; in others it begins at seven; of course, in very simple sort, as moving at a word, as beating time, as carrying a satchel on the back. At ten the work becomes more serious; there is wheeling, skirmishing, recovering, forming squares, deploying into line, and marching both in columns and in files. As they grow up, the pupils drill with arms; and in the fulness of their teens they practise firing at a mark. A field-day in the drill-ground is regarded by the scholars as a play-day. Every one is eager for a prize. The thing itself is nothing, for the glory is enough. Some magistrate of the republic gives away the prize; the Cantonal journal registers the fact; a hundred friends and neighbours praise the happy shot. To be a marksman in a village is to bear away the palm. Thus every male you meet above the age of seventeen is a soldier, ready in an hour to take the field.

Four weeks before the war broke out last year, General Dufour addressed from Bern a letter to the French Minister of War, Marshal Le Bœuf, on the defensive forces of his country. Bern is never likely to forget how often and how grossly France has violated Swiss neutrality in her wars with Germany and Italy. She feared that under stress of policy the third Napoleon might imitate the first; and when the project of a second railway through the alps, by way of the St. Gothard group—a project warmly backed in München and Berlin—was rousing France to jealousy, the aged Switzer took his pen and wrote these warning lines to Paris:—

'We have an army, more than a hundred thousand strong, well drilled and armed, supported by a landwehr, numbering very nearly a hundred thousand more. Our guns are ready for the field; our rifles are as good as we can find. We have our camps for tactics, and our schools for exercise. We have among us many military circles; but, beyond all these defences, we can count upon the national spirit in the heart of every citizen—a resolution to protect our independence and neutrality, let the storm break on us from whatever side it may.'

General Dufour is under rather than above the mark in counting the defensive forces of his country at two hundred thousand men.

The public force of Switzerland consists of three distinct lines:—1. Elite; 2. Reserve; 3. Landwehr. These are the official limits of the public force; in actual fact the whole republic is one school of arms.

A Switzer is officially a soldier from the hour

he enters on his twentieth year, and he remains officially a soldier till he enters on his forty-fifth year. From nineteen up to thirty-four he serves in the Elite; from thirty-four to forty he serves in the Reserve; from forty to forty-five he serves in the Landwehr. But a Switzer is a soldier long before he enters on his twentieth year, and is a soldier after he has passed his forty-fifth. At fourteen Switzers have been known to fight in line; and in the civil strife at Fribourg there were volunteers of seventy in the ranks. I hear of one case where an old man was rejected by his captain as too old; he trudged into another Canton, where he was rejected as a volunteer; and yet he followed his battalion to the field, and had a brisk encounter with the foe. In case of war against a foreign enemy old men and lads would flock in thousands to their flag.

No Switzer can escape from service after he attains his twentieth year. In one of these three armies he must find his place. In actual service some exceptions are allowed by law, but not on personal grounds, and only in the interests of the fighting power. No other claim to an exemption can be heard. All members of the Federal Council and the Cantonal Councils; pastors, priests, and masters in the public schools; some officers of the post, the railway, and the steamboat service; are exempt in virtue of their public duties. But the persons so exempted must have had their years of drill and shooting; they are soldiers out of uniform, and fit for duty, though they are not called upon to act. In case of need, they have the use of arms, and at a press would seize them for defence. And these exemptions are not made for life; they are not personal, but official; and they cease the moment office is given up. A priest and pastor may be said to stand apart, because their functions, which imply the rule, are held for life; but then the priest and pastor may be ordered in their sacred calling to attend the Federal armies to the field. All railway-porters, guards, and clerks are drilled in companies for the important work of transport, and in case of war the district General takes command, not only of the public roads, but of this powerful and efficient staff. Physicians, druggists, and horse-doctors, are relieved from bearing arms, but only if they march in their professional characters, and give the country more than bone and thew. A man who is the only son of a poor widow, or of aged parents, whom he has to keep, may claim to have his service lightened, so that he may not be taken far from home.

Under the Federal Constitution (voted in 1848—amended in 1866 and in 1871) the Federal army is composed of the several Cantonal forces. To the Elite, each Canton must constitute thirty men from every thousand souls; to the Reserve fifteen men from every thousand souls. In case of danger, the Confederation may dispose of the Landwehr also, and, indeed, of every male Switzer from the age of nineteen up to forty-five. Nor are these armies all. In war the ranks are swollen by volunteers; stout lads, who will not wait the legal age for fighting; grisly men, in whom the patriotic fire still burns. Nor is the female part to be forgotten in an estimate of the national powers of self-defence. In every public school the girls are trained to take their part. They learn to staunch the flow of blood; they learn to dress a gun-shot wound; they learn to nurse the sick. Swiss women have the lessons and the habits that would make them useful in a field of strife. They understand their civic rights. They know some chemistry, and they are quick at sewing, binding, dressing, and such medical arts. If need be, they can march in line, with knapsack on their backs, and keep up with their brothers night and day. In a defensive war, they could be used as scouts, as messengers, as nurses, and as teamsters; in a hundred things they would replace so many men. In fact, the fighting power of Switzerland, for purposes of home defence, is nearly that of all the population, male and female.

CHAPTER XXXII.

THE PUBLIC FORCE.

ONE army in the world is not deceptive in the lists of rank and file. For every Swiss name on paper there is here an active trooper drilled and armed. Nay, more; the companies and squadrons known at Bern and Thun are stronger in the field than in the books.

The first army—that of the Elite—consists of 70,088 effective men; divided into these six branches :—

1. Engineers	900 men.
2. Artillery	6,513
3. Cavalry	1,937
4. Carabineers	4,600
5. Infantry	55,994
6. Sanitary service	144
	70,088

But when these figures are confronted with the Cantonal lists, a great discrepancy appears;

and, strange to say, the difference is in favour of the League. The Cantonal details show a total force in the Elite of 85,000 men; some fifteen thousand more than on the books.

The second army—that of the Reserve—consists of 34,832 effective men; divided into these seven branches:—

1. Engineers	630 men.
2. Artillery	4,254
3. Cavalry	932
4. Carabineers	2,460
5. Infantry	26,448
6. Sanitary service	78
7. Armourers	30
	34,832

Comparing these lists in the War-office with the Cantonal returns, you note a second discrepancy in numbers, and again in favour of the actual strength. These Cantonal details show a total force in the Reserve of 45,000 men; ten thousand more than in the books.

These two armies—first and second army—constitute the Federal Forces, subject to the War Department. By law, each Canton must supply contingents to these Federal Forces; but instead of failing to supply the full amount of their contingents (like some other countries not far off) the Cantons yield their tale of men, and keep a vast reserve of strength at home; not less than five-and-twenty thousand men. In writing to Le Bœuf, Dufour spoke only of the Federal force — the paper army — which he counted roundly at a hundred thousand men. It stands a little over this amount.

Elite of all arms	70,088 men.
Reserve	34,832
Total Federal Force	104,920

The third army — Landwehr — is not under Federal control, except in time of war. The Cantons keep the regimental books; and it is only from the Cantonal reports that one can learn the full amount of strength. The latest Cantonal reports make the full force of the three embodied Swiss armies — Elite, Reserve, and Landwehr — 202,854 men.

To these large masses must be added all the Volunteers, both under military age and over military age; the youths who are already ripe; the greybeards who are also full of fight. From these two quarters, Switzerland might reckon on another hundred thousand men. In a defensive war, and none but a defensive war could ever be proposed, the country could rely upon a fighting force—all nearly ready for the field —of something like three hundred thousand men.

The army is composed of nine divisions, two roving brigades, and twenty-six detached companies. One division of artillery, and one division of cavalry, are in reserve. Each division, perfect in all arms, comprises:

1. The general staff of the division.
2. A company of guides.
3. A company of sappers and miners.
4. One brigade of artillery, with a park of guns.
5. Three brigades of infantry; each brigade of three regiments.
6. One brigade of carabineers.
7. Three ambulances (one for each infantry brigade).
8. Two squadrons of dragoons.

When the Landwehr are not called out, a Swiss division counts ten thousand men, eight hundred horses, eighteen guns.

The system of recruiting, drilling, and brigading, is that of Prussia, not of France; a local system, which combines in a brigade the men of one locality; so that in the camp a soldier feels at home, amongst his friends; his right and left hand files in service being the neighbours whom he knows and trusts; the men who would be near him in a snow-drift, at a fire, and in a flood. Each Canton has her drill-ground and her place of arms; and even those who wish to have one Federal army rather than twenty-five Cantonal armies, would not change this local character of each brigade. A company is a Commune under arms.

A French republican finds little that is democratic in the composition of this force. The rank and file have no discretion as to when and how they serve. A bugle calls, and they fall in. They have no voice in settling why they march, and whether they shall fight or not. They have nothing to say in the appointment of their officers, and they are not allowed to criticise the orders given. In putting on his uniform, a citizen becomes a soldier, and is subject to the articles of war. The Federal Council names a Commander-in-Chief; this officer is called his Excellency, like the President of the League; he takes the rank of General, which he gains a right to hold for life. In peace, the League is the supreme authority. She makes the articles of war. She founds and carries on the military schools. She summons camps for training and manœuvres to be formed. She names the staff, and keeps the only patronage in her hands. She orders out the troops, and gives them her directions where to march. Except so far as every branch of government must be an outgrowth of the popular mind, a Swiss army is an aristocracy, and the directing power bears less resemblance to a Paris Commune than to a Venetian Council of Ten.

The minister of War (who is, of course, a member of the Federal Council) corresponds with the military authorities of the several Cantons; gives them orders what to do, and how to do them; overhauls their rules and articles; and assigns the place and time for exercising the divisional troops. He goes to watch these troops afield; inspects their clothes and arms; and sees that every one is duly lodged and fed. He keeps an eye upon the powder, shot, and shell. He looks to horse and harness, cart and ambulance; but, most of all, he sees that every gun is clean and sound, and that the gunners know their trade. In time of peace, this minister is nearly as completely master of the Public Force as a commander-in-chief in time of war.

No jealousy is ever shown by Swiss democracy

of these great powers. In fact, the democrats of nearly every shade are clamouring for an increase of these public powers.

The General Staff consists of one hundred officers of rank; that is, of forty colonels, thirty lieutenant-colonels, and thirty majors; with a number, never fixed by law, of captains and lieutenants. There are separate staffs for the Engineers, the Artillery, the Judiciary, the Commissariat, and the Sanitary Service. Staff-appointments are extremely onerous, and only rich men can afford to hold them. Colonels rank with general officers in any other army. They command divisions and brigades, and form in fact the General Staff. Promotion goes by merit only. When the Federal Council want a commander-in-chief, they are not bound to think of those who bear the name of general, nor to take a man because he may have been a colonel half his life. No claim of either rank or seniority is heard. They take the best man they can find, and having given him power, they trust him to perform his duty to the state.

This General Staff conducts the military education of the people in the higher grades. Each Canton has the charge of teaching in the lower grades — the rank and file of Infantry and Chasseurs — especially the recruits; the League reserves the duty of instructing the superior arms, the Engineers, the Artillery, the Cavalry, and the Carabineers. For Infantry this period of instruction is at least thirty days; for Chasseurs at least thirty-seven days. For Engineers the period of instruction is at least forty-two days; for Artillery and Cavalry the same; for Carabineers thirty-five days. In after years, the men of the Elite are under arms five days a-year; those of the Reserve four days; and those of the Landwehr from one day to two days. The special arms must give a longer time to exercise and study in the field; but still the time seems short to critics who compare the raw material of a French or an Italian soldier with the Swiss. Such men forget that when a Switzer joins his flag he is a soldier ready made.

In carrying out her plan of teaching the superior grades the art of war, the League has founded six great schools.

1. A Central Military School at Thun, to which all officers appointed to the General Staff repair to be instructed in their duties.

2. A School of Officers at Thun, to which

all officers appointed to their regiments repair to be instructed in their duties.

3. A School of Cantonal Instruction, held in Basel, to which the infantry instructors come from every part of Switzerland to learn their duty, undergo inspection, and preserve a common rule.

4. A School for Young Officers, held at Solothurn and at St. Gallen, turn by turn, to which the several Cantons send their youths who have received commissions, and their youths who want commissions.

5. A Commissariat School, to which is joined a Medical and Ambulance School. This school is generally held at Thun.

6. A Shooting School, for officers who have to give instruction in their several Cantons at the butts.

The military centre of the League is Thun, in Canton Bern. The secondary points are Zürich, Frauenfeld, Aarau, Winterthur, Luzern, Luziensteig, Colombier, Payerne, Moudon, Bière, St. Maurice, and Bellinzona. Since the walls of Basel, Zürich, Bern, and Geneva, have been levelled, there are no great fortresses in Switzerland. Three works of caution have been left at

Bellinzona in Canton Ticino, at Luziensteig in Canton Graubünden, and St. Maurice in Canton Valais. No one thinks of these poor ramparts as defences; and the only question is, to what extent an enemy, in trying to force a passage through these alps, could count on meeting with a wall of steel and storm of lead in every pass?

'We are ready to protect our independence and neutrality, let the storm break on us from whatever side it may.'

Le Bœuf received these words in Paris on the twenty-sixth of June; and if the third Napoleon had been dreaming of a raid from Belfort into Southern Baden by the Basel bridge, as many people say, they were in time to make him pause and change his plan. A hundred thousand Switzers on Macmahon's flank would not have been such foes as any French officer could afford to leave behind. Events soon showed Napoleon that the Switzers were in better preparation for campaigning than the French.

CHAPTER XXXIII.

IN THE FIELD.

THE French declaration of war was given in Paris on the afternoon of Friday, July 15. A courier bore the challenge to Berlin that night. A message was despatched to Bern with very curt announcement that the war was morally declared; and on the Tuesday following, Wilhelm, King of Prussia, answered by a counter declaration from Berlin.

But faster than this message from St. Cloud came into Bern the news that France was moving to the front. On Friday news was wired to President Dubs that France was ready and would fight. That evening President Dubs convened his Council in hot haste.

Excepting Baden and Bavaria, no country had so much to fear from such a war as Switzerland. She lay between the combatants; the fighting must be at her doors, and might be on her soil.

When armies like the conquerors of Solferino and Sadowa rush upon each other, neutral states may chance to get some hurt, even if the great belligerents should try to spare them. How could President Dubs feel sure that France would try? Old Switzers can recall a time when France converted Switzerland into her battle-field, annexed the Canton Valais, occupied Geneva, wrung the Bishopric of Biel from Bern, and opened Basel to assault by seizing the strong passes of the Ergolz and the Birse. A Switzer knows by instinct that when France is on the war-path, Basel and Geneva are the foremost objects of her passionate desire.

The Savoy Question was unsettled. By the public law of Europe, certain parts of Savoy have been neutralized, and Switzerland enjoys the right of occupying them in time of war, not only in her own defence, but in the cause of general peace. So long as Savoy was Italian, no one raised a word against this public law. When Savoy passed from Italy to France, the King transferred his province with the rights attaching to it. In the treaty of Turin, it is expressly said, 'The King of Sardinia cedes the neutralized districts on the same conditions as he held them;' and this treaty adds that France will come to an understanding on this subject with the League and with the signatory powers. Napoleon had not kept his word. The Switzers wished this matter to remain within the sphere of public law; but Paris would not listen to their voice. French pride pretended to be hurt. How could a power like France permit her freedom on her own estate to be controlled by public law? She must be mistress in her own domain. No use to tell her she had taken Savoy subject to this public law. She was the sovereign judge of what she might and might not do. She would not listen to the Switzer's plea; and so this Savoy Question still lay open when the war broke out.

One hour after the President read his news from France, the Federal Council had agreed to call upon the Cantons to complete their regiments with men, arms, horses, guns, and all the stores and tools required in actual war. These orders had been scarcely sent along the wires to east and west—to Basel, Bellinzona, Chur, and Sion—ere this Federal Council, quickened by yet fiercer news from Paris, had agreed to call out five divisions of the First Army—the Elite; that is to say, the first, second, sixth, seventh, and ninth divisions, which were ordered to assemble in their several Cantons with the utmost speed. Full orders from the War Department followed these despatches to the Cantonal Councils and the Cantonal staffs. The first division, under Colonel Egtoff, was to throw itself upon Basel, to secure the bridge, and occupy the two banks of the Rhine. The second division, under Colonel Salis, was to move on Biel, and to hold the roads and streams from Nidau, Solothurn, and Delémont. The sixth division, under Colonel Stadler, was to rest on Bern, to succour and replace the second, should it prove too weak. The seventh division, under Colonel Isler, was to march on Fruenfeld, take up head-quarters in that town, and send out men to watch the narrows of the Rhine as nigh as Burg. The ninth division, under Colonel Schädler, was to cross by the St. Gothard, from Ticino, drop to Altdorf, and take up their quarters in Luzern.

The men were taken by surprise, if ever Switzers can be taken by surprise. An hour before the news from Bern came flashing into Aargau, Thurgau, Zürich, and St. Gallen, late on Friday night, not one in fifty knew that war was likely to break out; still less could he imagine that this tug of

Bonaparte with Bismarck was to call him under arms, and bring his training in the school and drill-ground to a sudden test. Yet every man was ready for the call.

On Saturday morning it was noised abroad in Aarau that the country was in danger; that the Federal Council had been sitting through the night; that men and guns were asked for in hot haste; and that the road to Basel was the line of march. By noon, strong squads of men were falling in before the new Town Hall. The district troops came pouring in. Some companies were quickly formed; their guns were drawn into the front; the cavalry rode up; the sappers, engineers, and guides got ready; officers were at their posts; and early in the afternoon the first Swiss troops were on the road. At midnight, as the Basel minster chimed the hour, these men of Aargau marched into that town. On Sunday morning, when the citizens awoke, they found these allies standing on their famous bridge; they felt that bridge was now made safe; and after service in the church they spent the summer day in helping these brave lads to chant the 'Wacht am Rhein.'

By Sunday night, the first division, Colonel

Egtoff, and the second division, Colonel Salis, were complete. The sixth and seventh divisions, under Colonel Stadler and Colonel Isler, were advancing, and by Tuesday they were also ready for the field. The ninth division, under Colonel Schädler, was assembling in the south at Bellinzona. All the five divisions called into the field on Friday night by messages from Bern, were under arms before the proclamation of war was issued in Berlin.

These five divisions of the first Swiss army, with their batteries of artillery, stood as follows:—

Staff and Guides	104 men	105 horses
First division	8,296	692
Second ,,	8,319	632
Sixth ,,	7,377	767
Seventh ,,	7,368	670
Ninth ,,	5,959	671
Total	37,423	3,541

These forces were supported by eleven batteries of artillery, mounting sixty-six field-pieces.

When the news that Bismarck had replied by war arrived in Bern on Tuesday night, a sitting of the National Assembly was convened, to name a General for the army and a chief of staff. All sovereign acts are done by the Assembly; but as every member of the Federal Council is an officer of the Assembly, not a voice was raised against this calling out of troops. The President had done his duty to the League.

Appoint a General! Every eye was fixed on General Dufour. This aged warrior fills in Bern the space once occupied in London by the Iron Duke. No name is known like his in every farm and shop; and as an act of deference to his age and name the Assembly called him to the chief command. But he declined the burden as beyond his strength. Dufour is eighty-five years old.

It was not easy to replace him; for the news which streamed along the wires from Paris grew each hour from bad to worse; and with a man like Grammont at the Foreign Office anything unseemly and unjust might be expected from the French. In early life Dufour had been a personal friend of Louis Napoleon; he was known to French marshals as a thorough soldier; and his presence in the field would almost count for a brigade. If Louis Napoleon and his generals were to be entreated, no man could entreat them with the presence of Dufour.

But, on the other side, the Federal Council

were not anxious to entreat the French. When Grammont sent them notice that the war was morally declared, expecting them to take an attitude of service to his master, they replied by a decree, announcing that 'any troops belonging to belligerent states, and whether they be regulars or volunteers, who violate the territories of the League, will be repelled by force.' They instantly forbade the export of arms and war material, and removed all stores and weapons from their frontier towns. They gave instructions to their magistrates to seize deserters and disarm any companies of soldiers on Swiss soil. They raised once more the Savoy Question; pressing what they felt to be their right and duty at St. Cloud. Napoleon was annoyed; he would not listen; he was busy with affairs. They notified the signing powers that they retained their rights intact; that when they judged it necessary in defence of their neutrality and independence they would occupy the parts of Savoy bordering on their lake. This note was laid before Napoleon at St. Cloud. He would not answer them with either yea or nay.

Alarmed by all these signs of French contempt for what concerned them in their dearest rights, the Leaguers turned their faces to the men who were the first afield, the men of Aargau; from whose ranks they chose an officer of high distinction in his craft, Hans Herzog, Colonel in the Federal army, as their chief. On Friday, Herzog came to Bern and took the usual oaths; on Saturday he was at Olten—his head-quarters, and the centre of the Swiss railways—where he issued his instructions to the troops. No gun had yet been fired, nor were the Zouaves swarming past the Rhine; yet every fore-post of the Swiss was pushed into the front. Colonel Egtoff, having occupied the bridge of Basel, struck into the gorges of the Birse and Ergolz, shutting up the two French gateways through the Jura mountains towards the Rhine. Col. Salis marched through Biel, made Delémont his head-quarters, and threw out his wings to Porrentruy and Laufen, close to France. Instead of resting on his arms at Bern, Colonel Stadler marched the sixth division to Munchenbuchsee, and spread his tents along the Emme and the Aar. From Frauenfeld, Colonel Isler moved the seventh division up to Frick, from which he sent out posts to Rheinfelden, near the edge of Basel-land. Colonel Schädler had now come up with the ninth division, and pitched his camps, with Bülach as head-quarters, from the Rhine, the Limmat, and the Töss. One regiment of foot, one battery of guns, one company each of sappers and dragoons, were sent from his division to Schaffhausen. The public forces now afield consisted of the following arms:

Staff officers	278 men
Engineers	492
Artillery	2,826
Cavalry	762
Carabineers	3,427
Infantry	29,538
	37,323

Such were the forces, such the dispositions, of the Swiss army only three days after war had been declared by Bismarck in Berlin.

News came to General Herzog, that the French were massing troops at Belfort; that orders had been sent to seize all carts and carriages in Alsace; and that the farmers of St. Louis, close to Basel, had been told to cut their grain, as camps on an enormous scale were soon to be established near the Rhine.

No bridge but that of Basel would have served the French to cross by. That of Strassburg was destroyed, and that of Mannheim was beyond their reach. His news inclined the Swiss Commander-in-chief to fear that General Douay would be ordered to advance on Basel, and he instantly prepared his troops on every point for actual war.

His first care was to organize his staff; his next to park and clear his guns. When these were done, he called the medical chief into his room, and formed two hospitals at each head-quarters—one for horses, one for wounded men. He ordered magazines of stores and clothes to be established in his rear, and then pushed up his forces to the front. Isler's division moved to Rheinfelden, and a second portion of Schädler's force was sent to occupy the neighbourhood of Schaffhausen. Plans for a campaign were studied on the theory of a French advance on Baden through the Swiss defiles. The Germans, massing under Maintz, were blowing up their bridges on the Kinzig, in the southern front of Kehl. They must be fearing an attack in force. The Baden roads were stript of men, and every town along the Rhine, from Constanz down to Rastadt, lay exposed to Zouave raids. If France was ready for her spring—as every one in Paris vaunted—he had only too much reason to believe that she would try to push across his lines, and take her enemy on his weakest side.

A troop of engineers dropt down the Rhine from Burg to Basel, studying every pass and point, and leaving companies of sappers at each bridge, with orders and materials to destroy it should an enemy appear in any strength. A staff of engineers went out to Bruderholz, and drew up plans for fortifying that important point. All railway companies were ordered to report their stock of engines, carriages, and open wagons, which, in case of need, might be impounded for the public service. These returns were quickly made.

  248 railway engines.
  911 carriages with 41,000 seats.
  1769 wagons; capable of carrying 11,000 horses.
  1925 open wagons.

Five new telegraphic stations were established, and in thirty-four stations service was arranged to be conducted through the night. With every arm prepared for duty, if the duty of resistance should be cast upon him, General Herzog listened for the boom of coming guns.

A fortnight passed in silence and amazement. Not a gun was fired in earnest. Not a Zouave crossed the Rhine. No enemy was seen from the Cathedral tower.

At length, the thunder broke—with peal on peal, and crash on crash. On Thursday, August 4, came Weissenburg; on Saturday, came Wörth and Speicheren; on Tuesday, August 14, came Courcelles; on Thursday, Mars la Tour; on Friday, Rezonville; on Saturday, Gravelotte. The storm of war rolled heavily towards the north and west; and then, all danger to the Cantons having passed away in the Teutonic victories, General Herzog reported that his operations might be closed; and in accordance with his hints, the camps were raised, the charges drawn, the gallant troops sent home.

CHAPTER XXXIV.

OUT AGAIN.

IN dead of winter those who had not served in that campaign were under arms in turn.

For six clear months—from August to January, from the battle of Gravelotte to the march of Bourbaki—the Switzers were at peace. No one imagined that the German armies would profane their soil. In every question that arose, Berlin was courteous, if not more.

When the Prussian Minister in Bern was asked if Bismarck would consent to Switzerland occupying Chablais and Fauciny, in accordance with her treaty rights, that Minister replied, 'Yes; occupy them; we approve.' The point was pressed a little more : 'If we should stay there?' 'We should still approve.' At one time there was trouble at Schaffhausen, and the Baden papers called for annexation of that awkward little slice of German land. 'You are accused of wishing for Schaffhausen,' said a member of the diplomatic body to the Prussian Minister in Bern. 'Of wishing for Schaffhausen!' laughed that officer; 'in place of trying to weaken Switzerland, we wish to round her off and strengthen her by northern Savoy.'

With Sedan there came a change. The very day the French republic was proclaimed in Paris, President Dubs held out his hand to her. 'We trust,' he said, 'to see the new republic, sister of our own, and born amidst so many troubles, give to France an honourable peace, and a long reign of liberty.' This haste of President Dubs was strongly blamed, both in the Chamber and the press. Why should a Switzer be the first to speak? 'No doubt,' the President replied, 'we have been swifter than the Cantons would have been; for instance, Appenzell, which has not yet had time to recognise the government of Louis-Philippe.' But the Federal Council, while exchanging blandishments with France, were bound to keep an eye on what was being done in Paris and in Tours. Gambetta would not yield the point of right and law; and left the Savoy Question open in his selfish interests; seeing, that if the Germans captured Lyons, it might be well for France to have the Savoy districts covered by a friendly State.

About the darkest time of winter a report arrived in Bern from Tours and Orleans, that a desperate effort would be made to strike the Rhine near Basel. Not a flying column, but an army of a hundred and fifty thousand men, conducted by the dashing and unscrupulous Bourbaki, was to force the Prussian camps, deliver Belfort, sweep across the Rhine, and carry fire and sword into the Fatherland. At first, nobody would accept this news. No soldier in his senses, said experienced officers of the staff, could dream of making such a raid; but whether he was sane or not, Bourbaki had accepted such a mission, and was on his way towards Belfort and the Rhine.

Already three brigades of the third division, under Colonel Aubert, were afield round Porrentruy, observing the affair at Belfort, and the lesser matters of the franc-tireurs and Garibaldians on the Lisaine. Colonel Aubert's troops were of the district, men who knew the roads, and were at home among the heaps of falling snow.

By night and day slight skirmishes took place between the franc-tireurs and German troops.

Some shells and bullets crossed the line. At Abévilliers and at Croix, small actions were exchanged; and in the second week of the new year, were followed by a running fight along the Lisaine, close to Héricourt and Montbéliard. As skirmish trod upon the heels of skirmish, Colonel Aubert, acting under his instructions from the War Department, which is wisely liberal with such officers, called out the whole array of local troops, and also sent to Bern for further aid in men and guns.

When President Schenk—who had succeeded Dubs—got certain news that France was marching towards the Rhine, he called his Council to confer. Their sitting was not long. Bourbaki's troops must come near Basel; they would find no other bridge by which to cross the Rhine; and the temptation to profane Swiss soil might prove too strong for men so desperately pushed by fortune. Everything was to be feared. Schenk hurried up some guns and men from Zürich, Thurgau, and Schaffhausen. He called into the field two full divisions of the army—third and fifth—and sent to General Herzog for advice. 'The danger,' wrote that General, 'seems to me much greater for the country now than when I took the command in July last. I see that one of two things must happen: either (1) that one of the two armies fighting at our doors may drive the other into our territory; or (2) that one of the two foreign generals, seeking for advantages against his rival which he cannot gain by lawful means, will violate our soil. In either case, the forces in the field are much too weak.' The President agreed with Herzog. In taking his command once more, General Herzog asked that the fourth division should be called into the field. He also asked for two batteries of mountain guns; one battery, 26, from Graubünden, and the second battery, 27, from Valais. These batteries were well prepared for winter service in a district lying under snow.

On Thursday, January 19, General Herzog quitted Bern to take up his command. The troops were new to him, and to each other. Not a man had been in actual camp before that week, and officers, as well as rank and file, had everything to learn. On Friday Herzog was at Basel, where he placed his fifth division under orders to secure the bridge, and guard the various passages of the Rhine where pontoons might be thrown across. Despatches followed him from Bern to

Basel, telling him, in substance, that the Federal Council hoped he would not need to arm the fourth division. Snatching up his pen he wrote, 'The failure of Bourbaki, and the fact that Prussian troops are edging his left flank, assure me of the end. The Germans mean to push the French, in either whole or part, across our frontier, and to put them out of service for the present war. I therefore beg once more, and in the strongest terms, for greater levies. If we are to do the work that lies before us, we must arm.' On Saturday, he heard of new successes by the Germans on the Lisaine; whereupon he ordered up his fifth division to the neighbourhood of Delémont, while he swung the various regiments of his third division round about Porrentruy. His own head-quarters were to be at Laufen. All his orders given, he was about to mount his horse, and ride to Laufen with his staff, when he received an order from the War Department to repair at once to Olten, where the Federal Minister of War was staying, and explain more fully why he wished to have the fourth division out. In fifteen minutes he had satisfied that Minister. Instructions were at once sent out; and Herzog, going back by train to Basel, leapt into his saddle, and departed for Laufen that winter night.

On Sunday morning he arrived, and having glanced at posts and papers, rode that day to Delémont. On Monday he pushed on for Porrentruy. The roads lay deep in snow; but all night long the crisp and silent air was broken by a crash of distant guns. French regiments were forming at Blamont, with eighteen pieces of artillery; a force, as Herzog learnt, which was designed to operate on Delle. The nearest way for them to march on Delle was through the Swiss defiles; and Colonel Aubert, with the third division, occupied these roads with orders to disarm the enemy should they break his lines. Would they submit to be disarmed? No one could tell; but if they hesitated at the summons, Aubert was to open fire.

All Sunday night, all Monday night, the Switzers lay upon the ground and listened for the noise of tramping feet. A world of snow and ice was heaped around their camps. The sky was clear, and bright with stars. Blamont was still. Afar off, in the mountain silence, they could catch the throb and clink of guns at Belfort; but the nearer masses of the French were all at peace, as though the wintry frost had seized and wrapt them in her silent shroud.

On Tuesday, Herzog rode along his lines from Porrentruy to Fahy, where he looked across the frontier into Abévilliers, and from Fahy to Damvant, where he looked across into Blamont. Eighteen hundred franc-tireurs were still in Blamont, under Colonel Bourras; but the Swiss commander, satisfied that these irregulars would not fall upon his posts, returned that night to Porrentruy, in order to be near the centre of events. His staff remained at Delémont in the rear. That night a person came across the border, who reported that the Germans were expecting an attack near Delle. At once the General leapt to horse, and rode to his advanced posts in the mountains, near the French hamlet of Boucourt, from whose outlook he could glance into the roads round Delle. He found his troops in good condition, stout of heart, well armed and clothed, in every point a credit to their flag. Across the border, lay a white and silent land.

On Thursday morning came in more decisive news. Bourbaki, foiled at every turn, was falling back upon Besançon; but the agile Prussians were at Dôle, between the town of Lyons and the French. Now Herzog saw that if this news were true, there was no chance of saving that French army from captivity, except by throwing it across the frontier into Switzerland.

CHAPTER XXXV.

A CROWNING SERVICE.

To General Herzog these results were no surprise; he had foreseen them from the first; and yet the vast proportions of the French disaster weighed upon his mind. A hundred thousand men, with arms and guns intact, but wanting food and fuel, shoes and shelter, stood before his little camp. A mighty and victorious foe was pressing on their flank and rear. He could not tell what men so desperate as that broken host might not attempt. His force was under twenty thousand men, and with a border line to guard extending from the Münster Thal to Val de Travers; yet he stood to meet them, if they crossed his borders, with the bearing of a man whose will must be obeyed.

Two days were spent by him in watching under arms. The cold was very sharp; the snow lay very deep; and, worse than all, a strong north wind swept down the Jura slopes in gusts. He dared not let his men lie still, and while he was compelled to wait events, he moved his troops about the mountain roads, at once to keep them warm and occupy their minds. Both officers and men were equal to their work. His troops were warmly clad and fully fed. At times they had to lodge in scanty sheds, and yet his lists of sick were very low. They marched up heights from which they could peep over into France, now white with winter, and could all but see into the streets of that once famous Héricourt, in scaling which their sires had won the pure white cross.

On Saturday morning (Jan. 28) the General heard from Colonel Grandjean, who was stationed at Les Verrières with some companies, that the Prussians were at Salins—that Bourbaki was at Bouclans, near Besançon—that the French army was disorganised—but that many of the officers imagined they could still retreat on Lyons by the mountain roads of Mouthe and St. Claud. Next came despatches from Colonel Aubert that the French were quitting Pont-de-Roide, which they had held in force, and were retreating on St. Hippolite and Maiche. These movements led him to suppose that some large masses of the

French might get away into the south, and that his troops would only have to deal with broken corps and separated regiments. If this were so, the danger of political conflicts would be lessened, while the fear of isolated fights would be increased. To meet these perils he must throw his forces into every ravine leading through the Jura, from the gates of Basel to Geneva, since the wandering bands of French might strike his lines at any point.

Some orders had been sent to Col. Aubert, when, near midnight, news came in from Col. Grandjean, at Les Verrières, that Bourbaki had killed himself; that a hundred and twenty thousand French were near Besançon; that the Prussians held the roads at Quingez and St. Vit; that every hope of falling back on Lyons was abandoned; and that all these broken hosts would soon be on his hands—to fight, if they would not submit—to feed and lodge, if they should pile their arms. A journal came by post, with telegrams from Versailles, announcing that Manteufel was driving Bourbaki and his broken troops along the left bank of the river Doubs.

The facts were clear at last; for whether

General Bourbaki was alive or dead—of which there seemed some doubt—a great part of his army had been caught. That army had no choice but either yield their arms or cross the frontier. Herzog felt that they would cross. At once he made his dispositions, so that every gorge and passage of the Jura should be held in force; the colonels having strict commands to fire into any body of troops, however large, which hesitated at a summons to disarm.

By long quick marches, such as German troops alone could match, the Swiss brigades were thrown along the range, from Bassecourt to the Sagne. These valleys in the Jura are not rich. A race of miners, quarry-men and charcoal-burners, dwell in villages far apart. Their life, at all times hard, is hardest in the winter months, when every road is buried under snow, and every lakelet is a bed of ice. Yet when these villagers saw the troops march in—young fellows who had left their cosy homes in Zürich and Schaffhausen, to defend their native soil from insult—they received them gladly in their houses, set before them what they had of best, and even turned their class-rooms into temporary camps.

While General Herzog was arranging either

to receive or to repel the French, Manteufel fell upon the routed army near Besançon, broke them at a shock, and forced them back into Pontarlier, whence they had one issue only—by the gorge of Fort de Joux, which led them straight upon the Swiss frontiers.

A single road leads out of Pontarlier eastward to St. Pierre la Cluse, where it forks out; one prong extending to Les Verrières and the Val de Travers, leading on to Neufchatel; the other prong deploying to the right by way of Jougne and Orbe to Canton Vaud. The railway line from Bern to Paris passes by the Val de Travers to Pontarlier, and this railway line being open, it was evident to Gen. Herzog that the French would try to enter by this shorter path. He therefore called in Col. Aubert from the neighbourhood of Blamont, swung his right wing round towards Neufchatel, and pushed as many men as he could muster down the Val de Travers. Fixing his staff at Neufchatel, he went in person to the frontier hamlet called Les Verrières, to be near the broken and unruly French.

Before him rose the battlements of La Cluse and Fort de Joux (two strongholds which the French have armed against the Switzers), covered with the wintry ice and snow; and close behind these frowning batteries lay some eighty thousand Frenchmen, mad with shame and hunger, who might rush at any moment on his guns. As yet, no word had come to tell him in what mood of mind they stood. He drew his forces into line, and waited, under those French guns, to hear what France would say.

On Tuesday he received a message from Pontarlier in the shape of a great train of sick and wounded men, which rolled into Les Verrières, drew up in the village, and awaited orders to go on. Four hundred men were in this train; but no one was in charge of it—no officer with the troops—no doctor with the sick. It was a lazaretto emptied on his camp. The train appeared to have been flung at him, as if to try his mettle. Should his feeling get the better of his judgment they might hope to see him yield on other points; but Herzog was too wise a soldier to give way in what was matter of the highest duty in his station at the sight of pain. Such flinging of their sick and wounded men into another country was a violation of the public law of Europe. Many of these sufferers seemed to be afflicted with contagious maladies — with typhus, measles, cholera—and General Herzog was amazed to think that any staff-officer should order such attempts upon his patience to be made. He sent his adjutant, Colonel Sieber, to the French head-quarters at Pontarlier to protest against such acts, and to demand the instant signing of an article preventing them at any future time. The French accepted his rebuke, excused their negligence, and signed two articles of agreement; one by which they bound themselves not to send over any soldiers who were suffering from contagious maladies; and a second, by which the Switzers were to arrest all fugitives and deliver them up at the nearest French posts.

A little after midnight (Wednesday morning, Feb. 1st) General Herzog was requested to receive Colonel Chevals, of the French staff, who came to him in the name of General Clinchant—acting for Bourbaki—to demand from the Swiss republic food and shelter for a brave and friendly army, which was forced by adverse fortune to seek a refuge on her soil. General Herzog named his first condition; a complete surrender — arms, guns, horses, men and officers. Colonel

Chevals came with full authority to treat, and the most pressing article was soon reduced to form. It ran:—

Article 1. The French army, seeking to pass into Swiss territory, lays down its arms, equipments, and munitions at the frontier.

But many other things were yet to be arranged; in all, ten articles had to be discussed; and these two soldiers sat up all the night reducing details into form. At four o'clock came news from Meudon, on the frontier, that heavy masses of French guns were pressing the Swiss Colonel Scherrer and his infantry, as though they meant to push across the frontier in defiance of his arms. At night, these guns had been sent forward from St. Pierre, and in the early watches of the morning an attempt was being made to get them on the other side. At once the General rose, and ordering out a whole brigade despatched them on the instant to repel the French.

Colonel Chevals saw with what a man he had to deal. By half-past four the treaty was complete. By five o'clock it was accepted and countersigned by General Clinchant, who was waiting in his carriage at the frontier, ready to drive in the moment he had signed his name.

Hardly was the paper signed before the multitude of men and guns came swarming over; General Clinchant first; close after him the general staff; and then the troops pell-mell, in broken, tipsy, and disordered ranks. With Clinchant and the staff drove strings of private carriages, with blinds and fastenings down. Then rolled in many vehicles: post-wagons, ambulances, military chests. Some Switzers were amused, and some were shocked, by what they saw. While not a few great officers had with them actresses, and golden plate, and costly claret and champagne, the rank and file had neither shoes nor over-coats to keep them warm in that high region, that inclement month. 'In worn-out shoes, in wooden clogs, and even with their feet bound up in rags, these wretched soldiers had to drag their rifles through the snow!' These words are General Herzog's words. At Meudon every man laid down his sword, his fusil, and his cartridge-box; until the heap of weapons rose into a hill. In all the French gave up two hundred and eighty-four pieces of artillery; sixty-three thousand four hundred and twelve fusils; fifty-three thousand seven hundred yatagans; three thousand and thirty bayonets; eight thousand and seventy swords. The powder and the bullets were not weighed and counted. Ten thousand six hundred and forty-nine horses were received. So ignorant were the French officers of their army, that they gave the numbers who came after them at forty-two thousand men. The actual numbers, when the Switzers counted them for food and beds, were 83,301.

The French came hustling over—frozen, tipsy, insubordinate; all arms in one wild welter; linesmen mixed with Zouaves; cavalry riding over guns and gunners; stores invaded and destroyed; no rank and step, no time and order; everybody pushing to the front; the four great army-corps convulsed into that worst kind of mob, a military mob. 'Your corps must gather to their standards,' cried the Swiss Commander; 'let your 15th corps assemble at Couvet, your 18th corps at Môtier, your 20th corps at Fleurier, your 24th corps at Travers.' General Borel, and other French officers, rode off to make these efforts in the cause of order. Here and there a regiment of the line, and part of the artillery, fell in; but not one company in five obeyed their captains. When the colonels rode among the crowd, they were received with yells and curses. Every one accused them of incompetence, and charged on them the sufferings and disasters of their troops. With pale, sad visage Borel rode into the Swiss headquarters to report that in the present temper of his countrymen no voice would be obeyed, unless that voice were backed by visible force.

Since the French could not keep order, Herzog placed the four French armies under charge of his own officers and troops. Despatching Col. Chouard to Fleurier, Col. Schrämli to Couvet, and Col. Cocatrix to Travers with their several regiments, he issued orders that the French should be directed on those villages in bodies of a thousand each, pell-mell, as they arrived at Meudon and laid down their arms. These orders were received with murmurs here and there; but still they were obeyed. A dozen Swiss soldiers with their pieces charged and bayonets fixed, sufficed to lead French columns of a thousand each; and General Herzog was surprised to find how patient and obedient these French soldiers could be when they saw that they were handled well. 'They saw at once,' he says, 'whether a troop-officer knew his duty.' Many of the French colonels asked his leave to go at once into the Cantons, separate from their troops.

A dangerous incident occurred.

On Thursday evening, late, a Prussian officer of Uhlans rode into La Verrières, with a letter from the Prussian General Schmeling, addressed to Gen. Clinchant, offering, on the part of Gen. Schmeling, to restore two thousand rifles taken from the French at Chaffois, on account of some irregularity in the form of capture. General Herzog gave his help to the accomplishment of a chivalrous act of war; and Clinchant having gratefully accepted the German soldier's offer, Herzog sent his orders to the forces stationed at the Col des Roches, near Locle, to receive the wagon-load of arms from the Prussian authorities. A squad of German soldiers brought this wagon to the Col des Roches, and having given it to the Switzers were returning to their camp, when they were fired upon by franctireurs, who had gone out and lay in ambush for them. Some of the squad were killed, some wounded, and the rest made prisoners, by an act of treachery, which Herzog afterwards described as 'a revolting abuse of the asylum offered to the French.' The Switzer in command at Locle was a man of steel. At once he seized the murderers, much to their surprise; at once he sent the German soldiers back to their own camp. A fever seized upon the French. They thought their franc-tireurs were right; and as this crime—if crime it were—was one committed on the soil of France, they claimed to judge them by their local law. To this demand the Switzers were obliged to yield. 'No man,' said General Herzog, with the indignation of a soldier, 'could foresee that a French tribunal would add to the original villany the still higher ignominy of liberating such assassins.'

This enormous host, demoralised by pride and misery, were received, disarmed, and led into their cantonments by less than twenty thousand citizen troops, without the forfeit of a single life.

The General who commanded the Swiss army through this crowning service speaks of rank and file with pride, though not without some drawbacks to his praise. The colonels, too, are satisfied with their men. Some Cantons have a quicker aptitude for war than others. Basel, Aargau, Bern, and Zürich, turn out men whom any soldier would be glad to lead. St. Gallen, Thurgau, and Luzern, come next. The men of Uri, Schwyz, and Unterwalden, make good soldiers; they are hardy, patient, brave; but badly taught and very poorly armed. In Canton Valais there is but one arm—the battery of mountain-guns; in every other branch this Canton falls below the mark. If Canton Vaud is better than Canton Valais, it is still a fact that La Suisse Romande is weaker in the field than even in the school. Canton Ticino is the worst of all; being bad in every branch alike. Her men are weak; her arms are old; her drill is loose; her officers are dolts.

The lessons learnt in these campaigns have quickened the desire for a more central system of recruitment and instruction, such as that adopted in the Federal pact.

Swiss Engineers receive the highest praise from General Herzog, who is not a man to say the word he does not mean. The gunners, sappers, guides, and carabineers, are also highly praised; except the gunners from Ticino, who are thoroughly condemned. And what about the rank and file—these weavers, tapsters, goldsmiths, herdsmen, farmers, what not—who are bugled from their beds, and sent into the field, alike in sultry heat and biting frost?

'They are a set of riff-raff,' says a foreign

soldier, as we sit in Bern beneath the limes, and watch the gold and pink fade slowly from the Jungfrau and the Blümlisalp; 'you could not call them soldiers by the side of French and English troops.'

'Did you see them when they came back from the Jura mountains?'

'Yes. Some weeks of camp had much improved them. They could walk in step, and hold their heads erect. Their skin was bronzed, their beards were grown, and they could tell an officer of rank by sight.'

'These fellows have good stuff in them, another foreign soldier says; 'they know what they are doing; they can read and write; great numbers of them speak two languages; and every man has been a soldier from his youth. They do not know how brave they are. With six months' fighting in the field, these fellows would be able to do anything they liked.'

'They might be able to defend their homes in case they were attacked,' remarks a Swiss professor with a pleasant irony of voice. 'There is another thing these men can do; when they put up their rifles they can earn their daily bread. Of course, they are not perfect; and we know of many things they cannot learn. You cannot teach them to forget their civic rights; you cannot teach them to adore a leader; you cannot teach them to prefer their colonel to their country. In these twenty thousand men you would not find the making of one Cæsar, though you might the making of a hundred William Tells.'

THE END.

London: STRANGEWAYS AND WALDEN, 28 Castle St. Leicester Sq.

www.ingramcontent.com/pod-product-compliance
Lightning Source LLC
Chambersburg PA
CBHW032043220426
43664CB00008B/840